Sir Thomas Fraser

The attack of fortresses in the future

Sir Thomas Fraser

The attack of fortresses in the future

ISBN/EAN: 9783337268954

Printed in Europe, USA, Canada, Australia, Japan

Cover: Foto ©Andreas Hilbeck / pixelio.de

More available books at **www.hansebooks.com**

ROYAL ENGINEER PRIZE ESSAY.

1876.

THE ATTACK OF FORTRESSES

IN

THE FUTURE.

BY

CAPTAIN T. FRASER, R.E.

[ENTERED AT STATIONERS' HALL.]

PRINTED FOR THE ROYAL ENGINEER INSTITUTE
AT THE CHISWICK PRESS.
1877.

CONDITIONS OF ESSAY FOR 1876.

"The Attack of Fortresses, in the future, taking into consideration the experience gained during the War of 1870-1."

The Essay should contain remarks on the following points, viz.:—

- a. The composition of the Artillery Siege Train, with observations on the ordnance best suited for attacking fortresses.
- b. The composition of the Engineer Siege Train, Parks, and Depôts, and the position of the latter.
- c. The use of wall pieces.
- d. Breaching by curved fire.
- e. The rate of fire of the guns in the Siege Batteries, and the supply of the necessary ammunition.
- f. Stationary Balloons.
- g. Observatories and telegraphic communication.
- h. Trench Railways.
- k. The organization and distribution of the working and covering parties.

The length of the Essay should not exceed 36 pages of the Professional Papers of the Corps of Royal Engineers.

LIST OF AUTHORS AND WORKS REFERRED TO IN THE ESSAY.

Boguslawski	Taktische Folgerungen aus dem Feldzuge, 1870-71. (Translated by Graham.)
Brialmont	La fortification à fossés secs, 1872.
Burgoyne.	Military Opinions of Sir J. F. Burgoyne.
Byland-Rheidt	Der indirecte Schuss mit Holgeschossen. (Translated by Oliver, in the Proceedings of the R. A. Institution, Jan. 1875.)
Cæsar	De Bello Gallico.
Decker	Der indirecte Schuss vor Strassburg. (Translated by Torkington.)
Geldern	Siége de Paris et de Belfort. (French translation by Grillon and Fritsch.)
Gillmore	Engineer and Artillery Operations against the Defences of Charleston, in U.S.A. Engineer Professional Paper No. 16.
Giornale d'Artilleria e Genio.	
Gatze, A.	Thatigkeit der deutschen ingenieur. (Vol. I., English by Graham and Martin.) (Vol. II., French by Grillon and Fritsch.)
Hohenlohe-Ingelfingen	Ideen über Belagerungen. (Translated by Clarke for the R. A. Institute, 1872.)
Jacqmin, F.	Les chemins de fer pendant la guerre de, 1870-71.
Jahresberichte über die Veranderungen und Fortschritte im Militairwesens.	
Jones	Sieges in Spain; by Sir J. T.
Josephus .	Ιουδαικης αρχαιολογιας ιστορια.
King, W. R.	Counterpoise Carriages and Platforms. (Washington, 1869.)

Lagrange .	Essai historique sur les Mines Militaires anciennes et modernes.
Livy .	Historiæ.
Militair Wochenblatt.	
Minutes of Proceedings of the Royal Artillery Institution. (M. P. R. A. I.)	
Mittheilungen über Gegenstände des Artillerie und Genie-Wesens.	
Müller, H. .	Die Entwickelung der Preuszischen Festungs und Belagerungs—Artillerie. (Part IV. Translated in the Intelligence Branch.)
Niel	Siége de Sebastopol.
Pasley	A Course of Elementary Fortification, by Sir C. W.
Paulus .	Die Cernirung von Metz, 1870.
Polybius .	Historia.
Professional Papers of the Corps of Royal Engineers. (P. P. R. E.)	
Revue d'Artillerie.	
Sace (Marshal)	Memoir on the Art of War ; extract in Valancey's essay on fortification.
Sebastopol .	Journal of the Operations conducted by the Corps of Royal Engineers.
Tiedemann .	Der Festung's-Krieg, 1870-71. (Translated by Tyler.)
Thiers and de Laurencie	La Défence de Belfort, 1870.
Thucydides .	De bello Peloponnesiaco.
Todleben .	Défense de Sebastopol.
Vinoy .	Le Siége de Paris, &c., 1870-1.
Viollet-le-Duc .	Mémoire sur la défense de Paris, 1870-71.
Wagner (Reinhold)	Geschichte der belagerung von Strassburg, 1870.
Do.	Grundriss der Fortification. (Translated by Schaw and Pilkington.)
Wolff (Paul) .	Geschichte der belagerung von Belfort, 1870-71.

REFERENCE TO CONTENTS.

SUBJECT.	PAGE.
ADVANTAGES of the garrison	12
,, attack	20-23
Alteration in trenches	74
Ammunition for a siege	51
,, in a battery	51, 52
Artillery, 1st position	56-59
,, 2nd position	76
BALLOONS	32-35
Batardeaux, demolition of	85
Batteries (Pl. vii.)	48
,, (Pl. x.)	62
,, approaches to	58
,, one night	62
,, requirements in	60
,, sites for	58
,, unexposed	59
Belfort (Pl. xviii.)	102
Besieging force	54
Blockade	2
Bombardment	3
Bombproofs	64-66
Breaching (Pl. xi.)	80
,, by direct fire	83
,, curved fire	79-85
,, limits to	83-87
Breech-loaders, advantages of	69
CARRIAGES, gun, disappearing	46, 47
Carriages, gun, high siege	48
,, ,, sliding	50
Cantonment of troops	23
Choice of attack	14, 15
Close attack necessary	87
Concealment of guns	62, 77

SUBJECT.	PAGE.
Communications	5
Counterscarp, demolition of	97
Covering troops	54, 72
Curved fire	41
DEFILADE of approaches	88
Difficulties of the besieged	9, 13
Direct fire	40, 77
Disposition of defenders' guns	19
Duties of siege troops	53
ELECTRIC lights	38
Embrasures, defects of	48
,, disuse of	50
Engineers	9
Extent of attack	71
External defence	6
FUSES, slow	84
GUNS, light trench	42
,, Gatling	40
Gun-cotton as a burster	84
Guard of the trenches	75, 76
HANDYSIDE'S engine	30
INDIRECT fire	57
Intermediate depôts	25
Investment, line of	7, 8
,, defence of	10, 11
KNAPSACKS, air	95
LOOK-OUT ports	70

b

SUBJECT.	PAGE.	SUBJECT.	PAGE.
Magazines, roofs of	65	Saps	88, 89
,, sites for	66	Sap-rollers	91
,, size of	51, 52	,, cotton stuffing for	91
Mines, war of	92	Screens, natural	57
,, cases for	96	,, artificial (Pl. ix.)	60, 62
,, respirators for	95		
,, ventilation of	94, 95	Security from interruption	17
Mining machines	96	Shelter trenches	75
Mortars, large portable	45	Shells, Palliser	84
,, earth	98	Siege plan	20-23
,, light	45	,, preparations for	23
Narrow parallels	75	Sights, raised	62
Nature of soil for works	18	,, telescopic	44
Night of arming	70	Sorties, objects of	13
		Splinterproofs	64
Objects of sorties	13, 14	Small galleries of descent	97
Observatories (Pl. vi.)	35	Stages of attack	99
,, concealed	36	Steam sappers	27
Offensive defence	19	Strassburg (Pl. iv.)	24
Opening fire	71	,, (Pl. xvii.)	102
		Strength of besieging force	54
Parallel, 1st	71-74	Surprise, attacks by	3
,, 2nd and 3rd	87		
Paris (Pl. i.)	4	Telegraphy, siege	36-38
,, (Pl. viii.)	58	Trains, siege, composition of	38
Park, artillery	25		
,, engineer	30, 31	Trains, siege, Artillery	39-46
Parks (Pl. iii.)	23	,, Engineer	52, 53
,, machinery for (Pl. v.)	31	Tramways, rail	27
,, organization of	30	,, wire	30
,, position of	24	,, plank	30
Penetration of shells	64	Transport by steam	16, 17
Platforms	67, 69	,, horse	27
Preparations for the siege	31	,, of guns	17, 50
		Trench depôts	25
Railway communications	6, 26	,, railways	28-30
Railways (Pl. ii.)	16		
,, trench	28-30	Wall-pieces	42-45
Reliefs, short	54	Working parties	73, 74

THE ATTACK OF FORTRESSES
IN
THE FUTURE.

318.

[*Forward.*]

" Actum, inquit, nihil est, nisi Pœno milite portas
Frangimus, et media vexillum pono Suburra."
Juv. Sat. x. 155.

THE part that fortresses have played in war may be traced in the history of all nations, and in these days, while the extent of practical operations has been largely increased, by the substitution of railways for roads as the main lines of communication of armies in the field, the number and choice of these lines has of necessity become more limited: a fact that seems to have given increased value to the fortresses which hold such lines, and has rendered their capture more than ever necessary. Hence fortress warfare seems likely to hold an important place in future campaigns, and of all the operations of war, none are more influenced by the changes in arms, and by the inventions of the age, than those of the attack and defence of fortresses.

In general, superiority in the field alone enables the assailant to attempt the capture of a fortress, while the object he has in view must, to a great extent, decide the mode of attack.

A fortress may be attacked—

1st. On account of the use the defender can make of it while held. *Reasons for attack.*

2nd. On account of the use to which the assailant can put it when taken.

Fortresses sometimes masked.

In the first case, if the fortress only threatens, without blocking the assailant's movements, and if time and troops can be spared, it may suffice to shut in, or even observe, the garrison. Thus in the war of 1870-71, the small fortress of Langres was masked only, because it lay to the south of the main operations of the war. More often, however, we may say, in the words ascribed to Hannibal, that "nothing is decisive but the fall of the place."

Methods of attack.

There are four methods to choose from, to effect this end, namely:—

1. Blockade.
2. Surprise, or assault by open force.
3. Bombardment.
4. Regular siege.

Blockade.

The first, which has been used since the earliest ages, is to enclose the place, so as to exclude all help from outside, and to wait for the exhaustion of the defenders' supplies.

In these days particularly, when the result of a campaign is so quickly decided, the method, unless chance favours it, is generally inapplicable; and yet we have in that of 1870-71, two of the most remarkable instances of its successful use. The first at Metz, where by the fortune of war, the garrison was suddenly increased ninefold, it could be foreseen that the resources that would, but for this, have lasted for months, could, under the circumstances, only hold out for weeks.[1] The second at Paris, where, though the living power of the city was under-estimated by the invader, no amount of foresight could have provided many months' supply for over two millions of inhabitants. In both these cases, therefore, a blockade was preferable, both on account of the certainty of the result, and because of the defensive capabilities of each. For the future, however, in the case of great capitals, the scheme of defence will

---

[1] There were provisions in Metz for 15,000 to 20,000 men for three months, though the supplies had been largely drawn upon before the investment.—TIEDEMANN.

generally be so vast, that a complete investment may be impossible. In these cases a modified investment is effected by merely occupying decisive fortified positions on the lines of sortie, so as to take them in flank : thus the greater part of the lines of approach will only be observed, and to secure a decisive result, a regular siege of one or more parts of the defences may have to be proceeded with.

2nd. The capture of a fortified place by surprise is a rare event; though an assault by open force may succeed when the assailants' superiority in arms is overwhelming—as, for instance, when our modern artillery is opposed to the obsolete guns and works of uncivilized races. Among well-armed nations the case is different, and the brilliant defence of Phalsburg in 1870-71, has shown how hopeless it is to make an unprepared assault, even against the weakest fortress, when manfully defended. *Surprise or assault.*

The third method, that of bombardment, is only likely to succeed in the case of a fortress of antiquated construction and armament, particularly when the defences include a town, exposed to the effects of the bombardment, and containing a civil population incapable of enduring its severity. *Bombardment.*

Of the fortresses captured in the war of 1870-71, at least sixteen fulfilled these conditions, and yielded to bombardment.

In cases where time presses, or when the result of a bombardment is uncertain, the most sure, and often the quickest method, is to proceed to a regular siege. Thus at Paris, Belfort, and Strassburg in 1870-71, some time, and a good deal of ammunition, were spent in fruitless bombardments. At the last place the bombardment was continued for three days by one hundred Prussian guns, besides those at Kehl (pl. iv.). *Regular siege.*

All experience, including the most recent, tends to show that a fortress, well armed and well found, if unhampered by its civil population, can only be captured by the fourth method, that of a regular siege. Thus even the antiquated works of Strassburg, ill armed and ill garrisoned, enclosing moreover a population completely exposed to the hostile artillery, were able to hold out till the German approaches almost reached the counterscarps; while Belfort yielded, for political reasons, after a lengthened contest, which might have been protracted far beyond the date of its surrender.

As the earlier stages of a regular siege include, for all practical purposes, the operations of a blockade and of a bombardment; while the conduct of the final assault, differs from that of an attack by open force, chiefly in the amount of preparation that is made to secure success; it will, it is thought, be sufficient to consider only the systematic attack of fortresses.

The Investment.

The siege being decided on, secrecy as to the intention, and speed in carrying out the investment, largely diminish the difficulties: while, to be the successful preliminary of a siege, it is all-important that the investment be complete; for it is not too much to say—with the lessons of Sebastopol before us—that a powerful fortress which can receive external help, is capable of a resistance almost without limit. Accordingly, the commander divides the intended zone of investment into sections, to each of which some unit of the force is detailed, and on which its march is directed. Thus, in 1870-71, at the investment of Paris (pl. 1.), the largest perhaps, and certainly one of the most perfectly executed operations of the kind, the Meuse army was directed on the north, its IVth Corps being ordered to extend to the Seine below the city, and the Guard Corps to occupy the region between the Creil and Soissons railways, whence the XIIth Corps had to extend to the Marne by Ville-Evrart, where it felt the right of the third army, which occupied the southern region of investment.

Movement of investing force.
In the advance, the cavalry, accompanied by horse artillery, takes the lead one or two marches in front, so as to conceal the march of the main body, and by the quickness of its movements to prevent the defender from drawing in supplies from the neighbourhood of the fortress, and from carrying out the

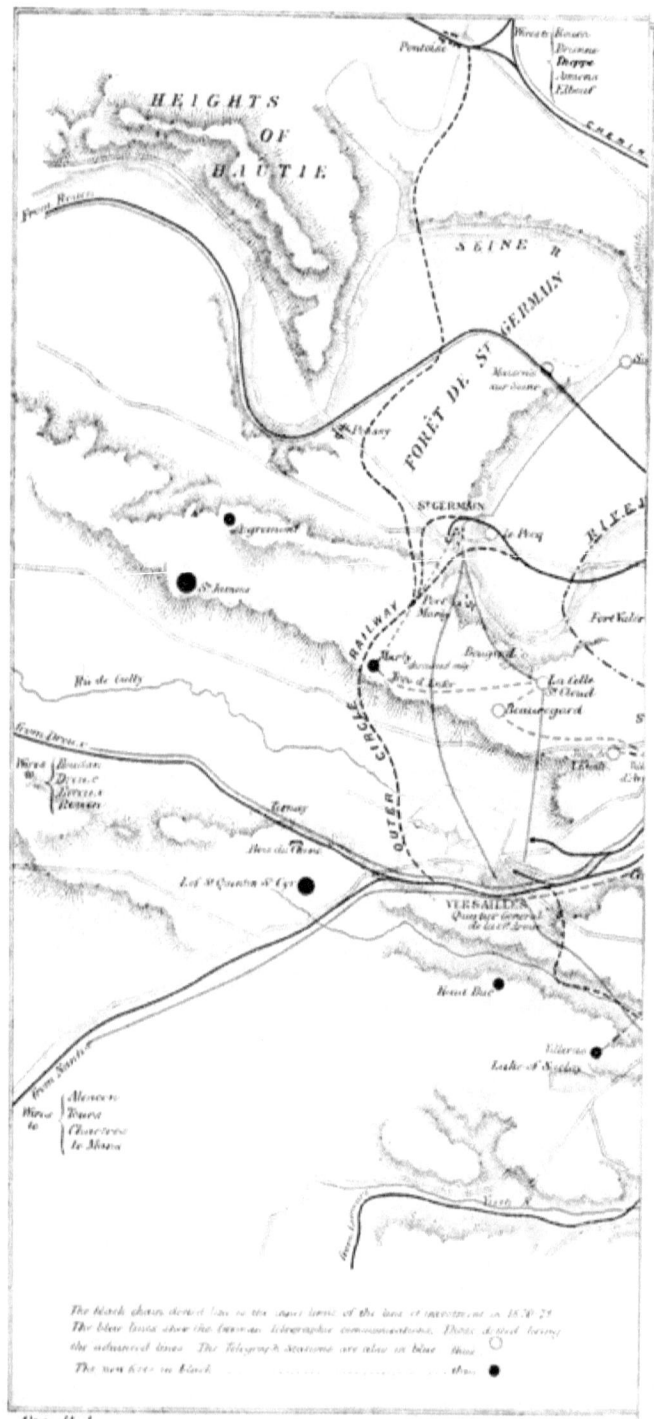

demolition of bridges and the destruction of communications. These advanced troops at once cut the telegraph wires leading into the city. In the case referred to, the fifth and sixth cavalry divisions of the XIIth Corps were pushed twenty-four hours in advance of the infantry, with orders to cross the Seine below Paris, and form a junction with the cavalry of the Vth Corps on the south.

At the moment of closing in on the place, the investing bodies are, of necessity, much exposed to attack from the field troops of the fortress, and their junction with each other is the first point to be secured. In the ordinary case of a fortress like Metz, astride a river, provision must be made for numerous bridges both up and down stream; and in the case of Paris, the difficulty of the assailant was further increased, by having, in addition, to deal with the Marne above, and the Oise below the city. Presuming, as is most likely, that all the bridges are destroyed, the first passages are effected by the pontoon trains, which accompany the advance of the cavalry; and on the arrival of the infantry divisions, their field companies of engineers at once proceed to throw boat, cask, or pile bridges across the river, and to protect them from hostile attempts. The engineers also break up the lines of railway leading into the fortress, so as to prevent the defenders from using them to get in supplies, as the French did at Thionville in 1870, where, though the investing force had taken up rails on the Luxembourg line, the garrison managed to repair it at night, and ran in sixty waggon-loads of food.[1] The engineers also drag the streams, to discover any telegraph wires laid down so as to communicate with the place. Thus at Paris, in 1870, a telegraph line, which communicated with Havre, was found in this way in the bed of the Seine.[2] An underground telegraph to Tours was also discovered; but though both were *tapped*, the messages, being in cypher, could not be read. They were, of course, cut.

Communication.

---

[1] Tiedemann.   [2] Gietze, p. 37.

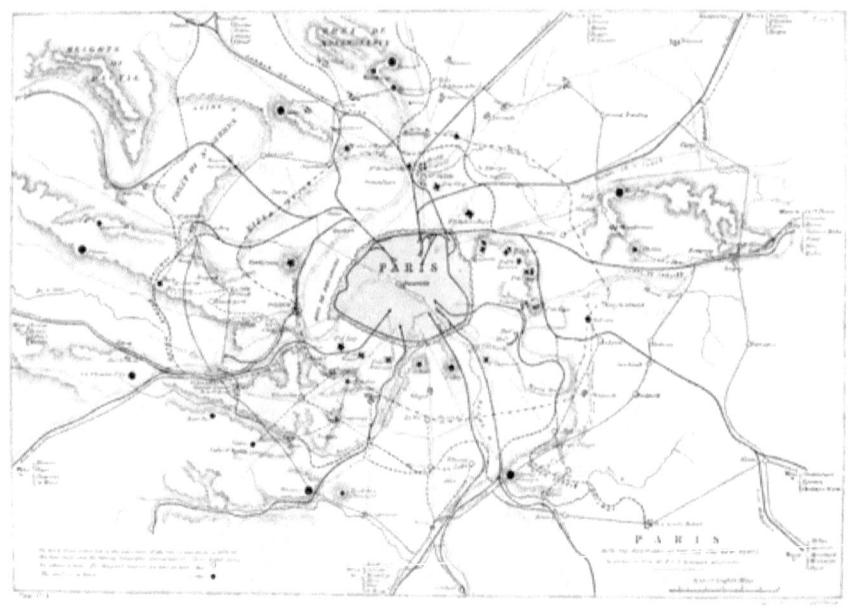

demolition of bridges and the destruction of communications. These advanced troops at once cut the telegraph wires leading into the city. In the case referred to, the fifth and sixth cavalry divisions of the XIIth Corps were pushed twenty-four hours in advance of the infantry, with orders to cross the Seine below Paris, and form a junction with the cavalry of the Vth Corps on the south.

At the moment of closing in on the place, the investing bodies are, of necessity, much exposed to attack from the field troops of the fortress, and their junction with each other is the first point to be secured. In the ordinary case of a fortress like Metz, astride a river, provision must be made for numerous bridges both up and down stream; and in the case of Paris, the difficulty of the assailant was further increased, by having, in addition, to deal with the Marne above, and the Oise below the city. Presuming, as is most likely, that all the bridges are destroyed, the first passages are effected by the pontoon trains, which accompany the advance of the cavalry; and on the arrival of the infantry divisions, their field companies of engineers at once proceed to throw boat, cask, or pile bridges across the river, and to protect them from hostile attempts. The engineers also break up the lines of railway leading into the fortress, so as to prevent the defenders from using them to get in supplies, as the French did at Thionville in 1870, where, though the investing force had taken up rails on the Luxembourg line, the garrison managed to repair it at night, and ran in sixty waggon-loads of food.[1] The engineers also drag the streams, to discover any telegraph wires laid down so as to communicate with the place. Thus at Paris, in 1870, a telegraph line, which communicated with Havre, was found in this way in the bed of the Seine.[2] An underground telegraph to Tours was also discovered; but though both were *tapped*, the messages, being in cypher, could not be read. They were, of course, cut.

Communication.

[1] Tiedemann. [2] Gætze, p. 37.

These services performed, two other duties must be at once proceeded with. The first, is the laying and organization of the field telegraph along the rear of the line of investment, and its connection, by semi-permanent lines, with the base of operations. The second, is to lose no time in commencing to make good important gaps in the lines of communication with the base; particularly with a view to the arrival of the siege trains. At Strassburg (1870) the Rhine railway bridge could not, it is true, have been easily made good during the siege; but the gap in the Mülhausen-Belfort line at Dannemarie, which might have been closed in a fortnight with the materials in the country, remained open till the end of the siege of Belfort; while but for it, the besieger, after the fall of Neu-Breisach, might have brought up his siege material by rail, almost into the trenches. At Paris too, to mention other instances, many of the Marne bridges on the Château-Thierry-Lagny line had been broken, and their restoration, as well as the turning of the blocked tunnel of Nanteuil, were works that proved of the utmost importance to the besieger.

While these things are being seen to, the investing bodies reconnoitre the sections they are told off to hold, and proceed to draw the line of investment round the fortress. The difficulties they have to encounter, depend, to a great extent, on the character of the commander of the place, and on the composition and strength of his troops. An active defender will make every effort to go out into the country, and prepare and hold defensive positions, which not only thrust out the line of investment, and so increase its length, but also cost the assailant both time and loss in carrying them; such actions cause the siege troops to realize their offensive power, and train them to fight. To frustrate this, and to deny the defender time to prepare, the assailant acts at once on the offensive, and endeavours to drive in the defender, till stopped by the guns of the place. The battle of the Alma (1854) was to a certain extent an instance of this, though it preceded the actual investment of the fortress; and at Belfort, in

External defence.

1870, though there was but a nucleus of good troops in the garrison,[1] the actual siege was delayed, for weeks, by the energetic occupation of villages, and other favourable localities in advance of the fortress; and by the obstinate stand that was made in them. In nearly all the other sieges of the war of 1870-71, the moral effect of recent defeats seems to have paralyzed, at the first, the offensive action of the defenders; besides which, as pointed out by Brialmont, there is the strongest evidence, that the French garrison instructions all tended to overrate the importance of the close attack, as compared with that of the more distant artillery contest.

Presuming that the investing force is equal to the undertaking, the earlier efforts of the garrison will, sooner or later, be overcome, and his outposts driven in to a distance of 1,000 to 1,500 yards from his works; after which, the assailant will be able to occupy positions astride the lines of approach to the fortress, and just beyond the limits of the effective range of the fire of the place.

It is evident that, in order to shorten the length of line to be held by the investing troops, the distance of this line from the place, should be as small as it can be; what it will be, must depend on the ground, as well as on the defender's numbers and the power of his guns; but we may observe that at Paris, where the defenders' artillery was in some cases more than usually powerful, the greater part of the first, or shooting, line, was at from 3,300 to 5,000 yards from the forts; that of the seventh division, on the north, which was well covered by walls and trenches, being at the former distance. *Position of investing line.*

On the subject there is, of course, some difference of opinion. Brunner considers that, when opposed to modern siege guns, the first, or shooting line, will be at about 6,000 yards, with outposts 2,000 to 3,500 yards from the works of the fortress. Hohenlohe thinks the latter will be from 2,100 to 3,700 yards from the defences. In the "Militair Wochenblatt"

[1] "The troops of the line were only one-sixth of the garrison."—WOLFF.

of April, 1873, it is considered that the line of advanced pickets—*i.e.* the first, or shooting line—will be at from 3,700 to 4,100 yards from the outer line of permanent works, while the latest writer on the subject,[1] places the line of investment of a large well-armed place, at a distance of from 3,270 to 4,366 yards from it.

Assuming from these expressions of opinion, that the inner limit of the zone of investment is not likely, at all events, to be less than 3,000 yards from the forts—beyond which distance, we may remark, the action of shrapnel is unimportant—we at once realize one of the changes brought about by rifled siege guns. For, judging from our experience at Sebastopol in 1854 (where the heights on which the allies first established themselves were 1,400 or 1,500 yards from the nearest defences), that, in the best days of smooth bore guns, the first line of investment might have been formed at 1,500 yards from the works instead of at 3,000 yards, as at present; we observe that in the case of a fortress having, for example, a diameter of 8,000 yards, the inner circumference of the zone of investment has now been increased from about twenty to twenty-five miles, or in the proportion of only four to five; while in a small place, with a diameter of 800 yards (about the diameter of Longdwy) its length would now be nearly doubled (fig. 14, pl. xix.); from which we further see that, as far as the necessity for increased extension is a difficulty, the difficulty of investing small fortresses has increased in these days in a greater proportion than in the case of large places.[2] This, however, is, in some degree, equalized, owing to the fact that the greater concavity of a small line of in-

[1] Translated from the German in the "Revue d'Artillerie," vol. viii. pp. 289-300, and 385-403.

[2] Thus the lines of investment round Paris and Metz (1870-1871) were respectively about 46 and 24 miles in extent, and were held in the first case by about 4,000, and in the second case by about 10,000 men to a mile. The investing force before Paris was actually inferior in numbers to the garrison; while before Metz it only exceeded the garrison in the proportion of 10 to 9.

vestment, permits of a more converging fire being brought to bear on a sortie.

This increased extent of ground to be held by an investing force would, under the old conditions,[1] have greatly increased the difficulty of the operation; at first sight, therefore, the defence appears to have gained considerably. Several causes, however, now combine to outweigh this apparent gain. *Difficulties of the besieged.*

1st. The garrison has now increased difficulty while acting on the offensive.

2nd. The great retaining power of the new arms, particularly of musketry, now enables an intrenched force to withstand the direct attack of greatly superior numbers.

3rd. The use of the telegraph enables the neighbouring bodies of investing troops to hurry up in support of the point attacked, in less time than it takes the garrison to advance over the wide space that separates the fortress from the line of investment, and to overcome the resistance of the lines of intrenchments.

4th. The questions of supply are now rendered much more easy of solution, by the use of the railways which, in Europe at least, converge on almost all the great fortresses.

Hence, provided that the investing force can hold its own long enough to intrench its positions, the results of the investments of Metz and Paris certainly justify the opinion that it can, now-a-days, retain a garrison of half, or even more than half, its own strength; while formerly it was held, that the proportion should be at least three to one: its success, however, will, at this stage, mainly depend on the extent to which, and the quickness with which, the ground can be prepared defensively, and the stronger the force employed, the earlier will it complete this work.

It is, of course, understood that the business of the actual siege cannot be carried on without largely increasing the ordinary strength of the engineers *Engineer siege companies required early.*

---

[1] Marshal Saxe, in writing on investments, considered (p. 143) it was necessary to have a battalion for every 100 paces of the line of investment.

with the army corps, to each of which only four companies are assigned in the field, and also that a body of siege artillery must be assembled, in order to work the siege guns; but, even at this stage, the engineer duties exclusive of the preparations for defence, are, as we have seen, so many and so onerous, that it is desirable to have the whole force of engineer troops destined for the siege ready at the beginning of the investment, to co-operate with the infantry[1] in the work of fortifying their positions, and preparing the communications.

Defence of lines of investment. The defence of lines of investment, should be considered as a special case of the problem of the defence of a position, and the method to be pursued should, in such case, follow the general arrangement as nearly as may be. This, for defensive purposes only, consists in having—1st, a line or chain of outposts and vedettes, often some miles to the front; 2nd, a shooting line, or first line of defence, on which the main stand is to be made; 3rd, one or more defensive positions in rear of the shooting line.

In the special case of an investment, the outposts can only be pushed forward, as far as the fire of the place permits. Hence the comparatively short distance between the outposts and the shooting line, deprives the latter of the usual amount of warning previous to attack. And here it is necessary to point out that the spots occupied by these outposts, are to be considered as weak posts of observation,[2] used to discover the first signs of a sortie, and to be abandoned before the outposts are compromised; for all recent experience shows that, owing to the extreme risk of retiring under fire, troops in force, once engaged, must fight where they stand. For this reason, the best ground to fight on is chosen for the shooting line, on which the outposts fall back early; and, where they make their stand, backed up by the

---

[1] As a matter of organization, the experience of the Germans seems to be, that the companies of technical troops (R. A. and R. E.) for the siege, should be attached to the divisions, rather than to an army corps.—HOHENLOHE, p. 5.

[2] "Weak outposts—strong shooting line."—BOGUSLAWSKI.

supports and reserves. It happens sometimes, that localities of importance must be included in the shooting line, between which and the works of the besieged, there is no cover for the outposts. These are, in such case, combined with the shooting line. To enable advanced outposts to hold out under the preliminary artillery fire, their positions should be strengthened, and these, as well as those of the shooting line, being exposed to the fire of siege, instead of field and position guns, should be provided with cover, which, both in its extent and in its power of resistance, should largely exceed that usually prepared for an ordinary position. Accordingly we find, in the investments of Metz and Paris, that a considerable use was made of sunken block-houses and field-casemates.[1]

Again, the circumstances of the case render it necessary, to retire the artillery into, or behind, the second line of investment, where they can be covered from the preponderating fire of the fortress; and whence they can co-operate in resisting a sortie, and can also, by direct or high angle fire, prevent a successful sortie from holding localities it may have captured in first line. Moreover, the uncertainty as to the time of the sortie makes the arrangements for the assembly of troops, and for mutual support, of extreme importance.

Lastly, the object of the investing troops being to repulse those of the garrison, while pursuit is denied them, owing to the nearness of the fortress; they are required to act purely on the defensive, provided the investing line can be held intact. For this reason, the lines of investment should be more nearly continuous than in the case of an ordinary position, and as offensive returns will, as a rule, only be made on a small scale, a very extended use should be made of obstacles, which indeed, during the first few days, will form the principal means of resisting night attacks;[2] for, while in preparing a position with a

Investment a passive defence.

---

[1] Cf. "R. E. Essay for 1875," p. 38, and plates. Also "P.P.R.E.," vol. xx., pp. 9 and 10.

[2] Cf. "R. E. Essay for 1875," pp. 38-40.

given amount of time to do it, systematic and extensive works can often be carried out; in the case we are considering, the day and even the hour of attack being uncertain, the works must at any moment be fit for use. Hence the character of these works is, of necessity, so irregular, that those of the Germans before Paris have been described as seeming, at first-sight, to be "the rude burrowing[1] of a horde of savages."

From the nature of the case, particularly with great fortresses, the zone of investment, considered as a defensive position, generally offers certain advantages and disadvantages. The extension of the suburbs that keeps pace with wealth, causes the neighbouring country to be much enclosed, built over, and wooded; and the great roads into the place which are the natural lines of advance for sorties, are, at the same time, the usual sites for the outlying villages and hamlets. On the other hand the roads, being mostly radial rather than lateral, great labour may often have to be bestowed by the investing army on their lateral communications; while, for tactical purposes little or no use can be made of the railways, though, as we shall notice further on, portions of these form iron mines of great value in the making of siege works.

Advantages of the garrison. The troops of the garrison benefit by certain special advantages, and suffer from special disadvantages.

The advantages are:—

1st. They can attack the investing troops at any time, with little warning, and from a secure base.

2nd. Having, in some cases, prepared the way by cannonading the defensive works of the besieger, they can advance rapidly, with a wide front, unimpeded by trains, with the infantry unencumbered with their packs, and supported moreover, for some distance, by the fire of the guns of the fortress.

3rd. They are, or should be, thoroughly acquainted with the ground, both for manœuvring purposes, and

---

[1] Viollet-le-Duc.

also for the use of high angle fire at long ranges, in order to disturb the besieger's cantonments.[1]

4th. They have peculiar facilities for making night attacks, a fact that obliges the investing troops to be constantly on the alert, and ready to assemble at their alarm posts; besides which, they must make nightly use of numerous patrols.

On the other hand the besieged cannot, from the nature of the case, execute any wide turning movement, and are driven to employ the front attack; and also, in the case of an ordinary sortie, they have the cheerless task of "coming out to go back again." *Disadvantages.*

We have now to consider what objects the garrison may hope to gain by attacking the lines of investment. *Objects of sorties.*

These objects are:—

1st. To check the progress of the works of investment; to hinder their approach to the fortress; and generally to delay the establishment of the investment, preparatory to the siege; as well as to accustom the untrained troops of the garrison to manœuvre in the field.

2nd. To relieve a too numerous garrison of some of its numbers, by breaking through with the surplus.

3rd. To act in concert with an external force, either a convoy, or a relieving army.

The difficulties in effecting the first object, plainly increase with the amount of time the investing force is allowed for preparation.

As regards the second, in the exceptional case of a garrison too large for the resources of the place—a circumstance which produced such fatal results at Metz in 1870—the object of a sortie, intended to break through, is not so easily attained as it seems to be; for, presuming that the investing lines are carried, the force, although it may have cut its way through, is without a base of operations, and is not likely to have succeeded in bringing out large trains; hence, if it be not in sufficient strength to have done this,

---

[1] Boguslawski mentions that the French shells so used at Paris, ranged 10,000 or 11,000 paces.

and also to pursue its advantage by rolling up the defensive lines of the besieger, it will probably itself fall a victim to attacks in flank, while in movement to secure a new base of operations. Thus, even had the French succeeded in breaking through the deep German formations before Metz, numbering, as we have already seen, about 10,000 men to the mile, and strongly intrenched, they would have found themselves at least four marches from any place they could have used as a base for supplies; and would, as we now learn, have been pursued by two cavalry divisions, and attacked by four army corps.[1] In fact, it is only where the effort is made in co-operation with a relieving army, that a garrison is likely to obtain decisive results against a strong investing force. While, therefore, this force is engaged in making up for its extension by strengthening its front, attempts to raise the siege may be anticipated, and must be provided against by a covering force, and sometimes also by defensive preparations; but in any case, by preventing the garrison from communicating with the external force, and organizing such joint action. The critical condition of the German Army before Paris in 1870, threatened as it was, up to the surrender of Metz, by the French Army of the Loire, is now a matter of history, and the protection afforded it by Von der Tann's detachment is in the recollection of everyone: while the attempts of Faidherbe and Bourbaki to raise the sieges of Peronne and Belfort, were, with difficulty, frustrated by the successful actions of the covering armies at Bapaume, and on the Lisaine.

CHOICE OF FRONTS TO BE ATTACKED.

Choice of attack.

The question "where to attack" must be considered from the moment the siege is thought of, and the Intelligence Department should provide all available information for the use of the besieger. From the moment of his arrival at the place, the problem is studied on the ground itself, by means of reconnais-

[1] Paulus.

sances, which, however, should not attract the attention of the garrison. For this there is generally no lack of time, owing to the necessary delays in getting up the siege trains, and preparing the siege materials.

Again, in the case of a vast fortress, instead of one attack, two or more may be decided on, while the first preliminaries of a siege may, in addition, be commenced on other points, with a view to distract and weaken the defender's resistance. The siege of Paris in 1870-71 gives examples of all these; for, while attacks were made on the southern and northern forts, a demonstration of intention to besiege was made against the advanced positions of Mont Avron and the eastern forts. As, however, the general arrangements of each operation will be similar, we propose to deal with one only. *There may be more than one attack.*

In deciding on the base of attack, the following points are to be considered in choosing the most fit field:— *Points affecting the choice.*

1. Which region of the investment will be most convenient for the arrival and parking of the siege trains, and siege material, and for the supply of the siege troops?

2. Which region is most secure from external interference by a relieving force?

3. Which will give the besieger the most favourable ground for attack?

The considerations as to the relative power of the different sections of the defences may be classed thus—

1. Against which section will a successful attack lead most directly to the final result?

2. To what extent do the works of each section command the distant foreground?

3. In what way do they bear on the ground close to them?

4. What support do they give to each other, and for the making of counter approaches; and to what extent, and in what spots are the latter practicable?

5. What is the nature and construction of the works composing the section, and their passive power of resistance?

Facilities for transport.

In considering the question of transport, it is impossible to forget the lesson we ourselves learned at Sebastopol in 1854-55, from the difficulty we experienced in transporting materials for the short distance that separated Balaclava from the trenches. Had Balaclava been a hundred miles from the fortress, we may safely say that, without a railway, the allies could not have carried on the siege. Since then the weight of the siege material, and especially of the ammunition, has largely increased. For example, at the siege of Strassburg in 1870, the Germans, we are told, fired sometimes as much as sixty tons of ammunition in a day.[1]

In one sense the work of the siege may be said to commence at the foundry or arsenal, the guns being but the funnels for distributing the iron stream that flows therefrom along the channels of communication.

Transport by steam.

Where a waterway, a great river, for instance, which steamers can use, is available from the base, it is, perhaps, the most convenient; without it, a railway is almost an absolute necessity for any great inland siege; hence there will be a strong reason for selecting, as the ground for attack, the point where the railway, or other communication from the base, most nearly approaches the fortress. Thus at Strassburg (pls. ii. and iv.) in 1870, the Weissemburg-Hagenau line ran through the besieger's works, and connected them with Germany. The besieger at Belfort, after the fall of Schlettstadt, had railway communication to Dannemarie from Strassburg; while, in the case of Paris, circumstances were much less favourable; for, though the direct line, Nancy-Châlons, was cleared by the taking of Toul on the 24th of September, it only approached the south-east portion of the capital; while the northern line through Metz, Mézières, and Rheims was closed by Montmédy, till the 14th of December. Hence, Lagny on the first-named line, and Nanteuil became the

---

[1] Fifteen tons at Paris according to Hohenlohe. "At Belfort the Germans fired 99,453 rounds, weighing about 2,200 tons, in 73 days, or over 1,360 rounds a day."—WOLFF, Appendix, p. 8.

RAILWAYS IN THE WAR
OF
1870-71.

great points of debarkation; and at the latter, the
artillery and engineer siege trains had to be unloaded, and conveyed thence, by road, to the parks
at Villecoublay, a distance of nearly forty miles. For
this service the artillery alone required 900 horsed
waggons. This circumstance delayed the siege operations for many weeks, and would have been very
serious, had the invader depended for success on
the siege alone.

In addition, as the assailant will be in greater
strength where the siege takes place, than elsewhere
along the line of investment, the nearness of the
communication will be most valuable here for the
provisioning of the troops.[1] Indeed, the business
of supply alone, in a large operation, is a matter of
extraordinary difficulty, if dependent on roads only:
so much so, that before Paris, even with two railways,
the transport of siege material had often to be stopped
on account of the requirements of the troops. Next
to the railways, the nature and condition of the roads
must be considered; for, however convenient the
former may be, large use must always be made of
the latter: these should also be looked to with a
view to a possible retreat. Other points are the
local resources in the way of wood and water; the
relative healthiness of the region, particularly in
view of a protracted siege; the extent to which the
siege troops can be housed in outlying villages, &c.;
and the distances within which brushwood and timber
for siege purposes can be procured.

The security of the siege troops from external *Security from
interruption, is of course very important. Thus the interruption.*
site of the German attack of Belfort in 1870-71, had
the advantage of being on the side furthest removed
from the probable advance of a relieving force.[2]

---

[1] A train of 60 railway waggons carries the supplies for a day for
60,000 men and 12,000 horses. Such a train can seldom travel
more than 180 miles in 24 hours; only one can be run every hour,
and it takes about 10 hours to load, and the same to unload it. A
heavy siege gun, completely equipped, and with 500 rounds, requires
about five trucks. See M. P. R. A. I., December, 1871, p. 27.

[2] Cf. Royal Engineer Essay of 1875, pt. i.

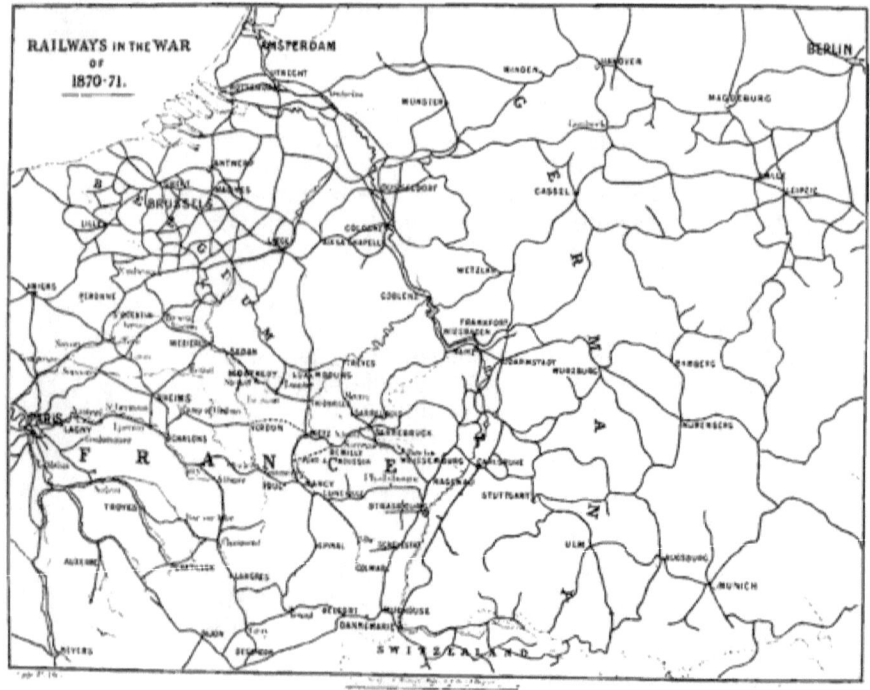

great points of debarkation; and at the latter, the artillery and engineer siege trains had to be unloaded, and conveyed thence, by road, to the parks at Villecoublay, a distance of nearly forty miles. For this service the artillery alone required 900 horsed waggons. This circumstance delayed the siege operations for many weeks, and would have been very serious, had the invader depended for success on the siege alone.

In addition, as the assailant will be in greater strength where the siege takes place, than elsewhere along the line of investment, the nearness of the communication will be most valuable here for the provisioning of the troops.[1] Indeed, the business of supply alone, in a large operation, is a matter of extraordinary difficulty, if dependent on roads only: so much so, that before Paris, even with two railways, the transport of siege material had often to be stopped on account of the requirements of the troops. Next to the railways, the nature and condition of the roads must be considered; for, however convenient the former may be, large use must always be made of the latter: these should also be looked to with a view to a possible retreat. Other points are the local resources in the way of wood and water; the relative healthiness of the region, particularly in view of a protracted siege; the extent to which the siege troops can be housed in outlying villages, &c.; and the distances within which brushwood and timber for siege purposes can be procured.

Security from interruption. The security of the siege troops from external interruption, is of course very important. Thus the site of the German attack of Belfort in 1870-71, had the advantage of being on the side furthest removed from the probable advance of a relieving force.[2]

---

[1] A train of 60 railway waggons carries the supplies for a day for 60,000 men and 12,000 horses. Such a train can seldom travel more than 180 miles in 24 hours; only one can be run every hour, and it takes about 10 hours to load, and the same to unload it. A heavy siege gun, completely equipped, and with 500 rounds, requires about five trucks. See M. P. R. A. I., December, 1871, p. 27.

[2] Cf. Royal Engineer Essay of 1875. pl. i.

Ground to be favourable for a siege, should afford the investing force strong defensible positions on the flanks of the attack. Its situation should, if possible, command the site of the works to be attacked, as was notably the case before the southern forts of Paris, and before St. Denis in 1870-71. It should either by its form, or the cover upon it, aid the concealment of the first siege batteries and approaches. It should possess suitable and secure positions for the parks, and should, as far as may be, cover the approaches from them to the front.

Nature of the soil. It is desirable too that the soil, where trench-work must be done, should be neither rocky nor wet. The difficulties of rocky soil were experienced both by the allies at the siege of Sebastopol, and by the Germans before Belfort, so that blasting had to be resorted to; and in the latter case only a width of three or four feet could be given to the approaches; while at Thionville, in 1870, the Germans opened part of the first parallel in ploughed land, the deep furrows of which ran perpendicularly to the trench, and these (acting as drains) soon filled the excavation, which had to be abandoned.

Aim directly at the final result. As regards the fortress, it will often be best to attack a strong section, if, by so doing, we can arrive more directly at our object. Thus at Belfort the attack of Fort la Miotte, which was the easier, was rejected for that on the citadel, because, had the former been taken, a further attack of the citadel would have been required. Similarly at Paris, though the attack of St. Denis was in itself easy, the further advance to the enceinte would have been attended with great difficulties; while an attack on Valérien, which its isolated position suggested, would, if successful, have left the assailant with a broad river to cross, before advancing against the city. The attack of the line Issy-Montrouge, on the contrary, led most directly to the final object (pls. viii. and xviii.).

Defensive field of fire. The extent to which the fire of the defences can command the besieger's works, will be considered at first by means of the plans of the fortress in possession of the besieger, who will correct them by observations on the ground; these will also enable him to judge how far he will have to deal with collateral works.

There is, in addition, another point, the importance of which can hardly be over estimated, and which is the natural sequence of the adoption of detached forts, instead of continuous lines, namely, the increasing use of the system of offensive defence, which received so great a development at Sebastopol, and which the French used, in a measure, both at Belfort and Paris. Formerly, in attacking a continuous enceinte, counter approaches for infantry were occasionally attempted, but even the imperfect use made of detached forts in 1870-71, shows that an active defender will, for the future, chiefly use the forts as a line of keeps and observatories in a great defensive position; the forts themselves only mounting such guns as can be thoroughly well covered; while a number of their guns, as well as a proportion of the artillery from works not engaged, will be posted in siege batteries, between, or just in rear of the line of forts, and connected with them by trenches; in rear of these trenches, fresh batteries can be made, into which to shift any guns that may be too hardly pressed by the attack. True, the extent of sites for such batteries is much more limited in depth than in the case of the assailant, but still, a large area is available. There can, it is thought, be little doubt but that the size of the new German detached forts at Strassburg, in which provision is made for only fourteen or sixteen guns on siege carriages, has been decided with a view to such a system of defence, and that, small though they be, they will prove equal to the requirements of the case. An increase of mobility in the fortress artillery is dependent on the natures of carriages on which the guns are mounted: in fact, the carriages that best suit the purpose of the besieger will, in most cases, be the best for the besieged. The contrary will be the case, chiefly during the close defence, and particularly, when *depression* may be required; as guns on high carriages, *en barbette*, are then much exposed, and should be withdrawn behind emplacements in the interior of the works, and screened by their parapets, or into screened external batteries; while the advantages of direct fire can still be retained by using guns which recoil under cover, or those in plated casemates or turrets, or those in flank haxos, the embrasures of which are not exposed to artillery fire.

The difficulty the besieger encounters, in dealing with such a system of defence, is that, while for the distant artillery contest, the defender's guns in these external batteries, and behind the parapets of the works, compete with his on something like equal terms; a portion of the fire of the forts can, to a great extent, be reserved till the period of the close attack; either by shifting guns into unseen positions for indirect fire; or by methods of mounting and protection which permit of the use of direct fire, when their command gives the guns considerable advantage. Hence, in deciding the question, the besieger must not only take into account the means of resistance that are known to exist, but also those it is possible or likely that the defender may develop.

The siege plan. With regard to the details of the permanent works, little more than what is known from the plans can be ascertained at this stage, because the fire of the fortress hinders the approach of reconnaissances. All these points having been weighed, a decision must be come to as to the section of the fortress to be attacked; and taking all the data into account, the commanding engineer submits a plan of attack to the commander of the siege troops. This plan can only indicate generally the scheme of the attack, its probable extent, and its ultimate direction, as well as the general positions of the siege parks, and of the intermediate depôts. The positions of the parks, in particular, require to be decided on early, so as to organize the transport of materials.

The sites for the parks decided on early.

Advantages of the attack. We will now consider the main points of difference in the conduct of sieges under the old and new conditions. And first, as to the advantages of the attack over the defence.

As in the field, so at a siege, the assailant has always had, and to a certain extent retains—

1st. The advantage of the initiative.

2nd. The power to judge beforehand of the defender's means of resistance, and to regulate his own accordingly, though in a much less degree in the case of improvised defences.[1]

3rd. The benefit of a well-defined objective before him, about which he should have some previous knowledge, while the defender has first to discover, and then to deal with works, about which he must now be more than ever ignorant, particularly as the assailant is no longer forced, as of old, to place his batteries on sites which the defender might foresee would be occupied.

4th. The means of availing himself of the best and newest engines of war, being in general only limited by weight, while the cost, and permanent nature of fortifications, prevent their being constantly modified, in accordance with the changes in arms. In addition, the number of guns required to arm many fortresses is so great, that economy may prevent their being entirely armed with the newest artillery, though a portion of their guns will often be heavier than anything the besieger can oppose to them.[2]

5th. Tactically speaking, the besieger has, further, had advantages which have constantly increased with the increased range and power of the arms in use. At first, when men fought hand to hand, there was nothing to counterbalance the advantages of the defensive; but as soon as missiles came to be used, the attack began to gain new powers; in the first place, the power of showing the wider front, and thereby enveloping the defender along the whole line of his defences; and in the second, of having a distinct point of attack, on which to concentrate the effects of his

---

[1] At Sebastopol, the scheme of the Russian defence could not have been foreseen, a fact that greatly increased the difficulty of the siege.

[2] With the exception of a few 21c. guns, the 7 in. B. L. R., the 64 pr. M. L. R., and the 15c. ring guns are the most powerful now on land fronts.

more widely distributed engines. Of these advantages the latter cannot be entirely lost by the assailant, except through want of judgment; while the former is dependent on the extent of the defences, and is most marked when the progress of fortification has fallen, as it sometimes may, behind that of artillery, owing to rapid improvements in the latter.

No more remarkable instances of this are to be found, than in the war of 1870-71, in which, in addition to moral and other disadvantages,[1] a number of small fortresses of antiquated construction, suddenly found themselves opposed to an artillery which, in power and range, as far surpassed the guns of their date, as these latter did the catapults and mangonels of earlier ages.

In such cases the result could not be doubtful. But even when the advantages are less marked, improvements in construction alone, apart from increased extent, will not deprive the attack of this superiority. For if, to fix our ideas, we consider that the modern siege gun is as effective against modern works at 2,000 yards, as smooth-bore guns were at 500 yards, against the works of their day; we see that, in a small fortress having a diameter of 800 yards, the arc of attack, so to speak (fig. 14), which was formerly little more than double that of the defence, has now become six times as great; while, in the case of a fortress of 8,000 yards diameter, the arc of a modern attack is only greater by a third than that of the defence, and has, as compared with that at the old distance, increased only in the ratio of nine to twelve: thus, to take two extreme cases, we see at the siege of Toul (1870-71), the German batteries occupying a complete semicircle, and distant about a mile from the place; while, if we turn to the operation against the southern forts of Paris, we notice that the arc has, perforce, become a

---

[1] Among others, the inferiority of their armaments, the want of ammunition, and the absence of technical troops. Thus many of the fortresses in 1870-71 were chiefly armed with smooth-bores. Again, at the time of the surrender of Belfort, the supply of rifled shells had run low; in Toul hardly any were left: while at Strassburg there were only sixteen sappers, and but few gunners in the place.

GERMAN ENGINEER PARK SOUTH OF PARIS, 1870-71.

straight line; and we find the assailant, while retaining, to some extent, his power of concentration, deprived of his enveloping power, as regards the whole line of defence.

We conclude therefore, that under the new state of things, the power of resistance of small fortresses has relatively decreased: the more so as their defences are now exposed to be bombarded *in reverse*, by the far ranging guns of the siege trains.

PREPARATIONS FOR THE SIEGE.

When the army of investment has succeeded in enclosing the fortress, has intrenched itself against the sorties of the garrison, has taken measures to guard itself from external interruption, and when the point of attack has been decided on, the business of the siege begins. The question of sheltering the siege troops must of course depend on circumstances. If there be many villages at hand, and available, it may suffice, in great measure, to use them. When, however, the troops have to march to and fro some miles to the siege works, the fatigue of doing so, may seriously interfere with the execution of these works; or, if the cantonments be so situated as to hinder their rapid assembly, their power of resisting sorties may be diminished;[1] hence it may be necessary to make huts for a portion of them, as was done in many instances during the war of 1870-71, as, for example, at Gonesse, north of Paris; at Metz; and in the wood of Bosmont, before Belfort; though in most cases the villages sufficed. At Sebastopol, on the other hand, shelter had to be provided for almost all the troops, and the work of sheltering them was so onerous, that the siege works had to be left undone while it was being carried out.

Cantonment of troops.

[1] "In the instructions for the siege of Belfort in 1870, it was laid down that the cantonments were to be such as to permit of the men getting under arms in five minutes."—WOLFF, Appendix, p. 6.

Positions of the parks.

While the troops are being housed, the exact positions of the artillery and engineer parks are decided on, and the organization of them begun. Owing to the fatal consequences that might befall the whole operation, in case a successful sortie could reach them, and destroy their contents; it is necessary, in choosing sites for them, to fix on spots in rear of the defences of investment, and out of sight of the fortress. So placed, they will generally be at such a distance from the latter, as to be secure from the effects of random fire.[1]

The distance of the artillery and engineer parks from the place, will probably be, for the former $3\frac{1}{2}$ to $4\frac{1}{2}$, and for the latter 3 to $3\frac{1}{2}$ miles; but must depend on circumstances: at the attack on the northern forts of Paris, where the ground was somewhat open, both the siege parks seem to have been near the Patte d'Oie, east of Gonesse, and about 8,700 yards from the forts; while, for the southern attack, the parks were at Villa-Coublay (pls. i. and iii.), distant about 5,500 yards from the works, but covered by the wood of Clamart. Some uneasiness was felt about the position of these last, and considerable labour was spent in intrenching them.[2]

Again, at Strassburg (pl. iv.) the artillery park north of Mundolsheim was 6,300 yards, and the engineer park at Souffelsweirheim was about 4,700 yards from the place.

In the attacks of the smaller places in 1870-71, it was possible, without risk, to place the parks much closer. Thus, before Mézières, the engineer park was at Francheville, 3,500 yards from the fortress, while at Soissons, the artillery and engineer parks were respectively distant 4,100 and 3,300 yards from the place, and on the same road.

An Austrian writer[3] on the future of sieges has

---

[1] According to Tiedemann, the French shells from Strassburg, fired the village of Mittelhausbergen, distant 4,600 yards (pl. iv.).

[2] Brunner suggests a distance of 6,000 yards from the most advanced works, for the siege camp, and parks; but recommends that the main magazine for the artillery park be 8,000 yards back (p. 19).

[3] In the "Militair Wochenblatt," for April, 1873.

Positions of the parks.

While the troops are being housed, the exact positions of the artillery and engineer parks are decided on, and the organization of them begun. Owing to the fatal consequences that might befall the whole operation, in case a successful sortie could reach them, and destroy their contents; it is necessary, in choosing sites for them, to fix on spots in rear of the defences of investment, and out of sight of the fortress. So placed, they will generally be at such a distance from the latter, as to be secure from the effects of random fire.[1]

The distance of the artillery and engineer parks from the place, will probably be, for the former $3\frac{1}{2}$ to $4\frac{1}{2}$, and for the latter 3 to $3\frac{1}{2}$ miles; but must depend on circumstances: at the attack on the northern forts of Paris, where the ground was somewhat open, both the siege parks seem to have been near the Patte d'Oie, east of Gonesse, and about 8,700 yards from the forts; while, for the southern attack, the parks were at Villa-Coublay (pls. i. and iii.), distant about 5,500 yards from the works, but covered by the wood of Clamart. Some uneasiness was felt about the position of these last, and considerable labour was spent in intrenching them.[2]

Again, at Strassburg (pl. iv.) the artillery park north of Mundolsheim was 6,300 yards, and the engineer park at Souffelsweirheim was about 4,700 yards from the place.

In the attacks of the smaller places in 1870-71, it was possible, without risk, to place the parks much closer. Thus, before Mézières, the engineer park was at Francheville, 3,500 yards from the fortress, while at Soissons, the artillery and engineer parks were respectively distant 4,100 and 3,300 yards from the place, and on the same road.

An Austrian writer[3] on the future of sieges has

[1] According to Tiedemann, the French shells from Strassburg, fired the village of Mittelhausbergen, distant 4,600 yards (pl. iv.).

[2] Brunner suggests a distance of 6,000 yards from the most advanced works, for the siege camp, and parks; but recommends that the main magazine for the artillery park be 8,000 yards back (p. 19).

[3] In the "Militair Wochenblatt," for April, 1873.

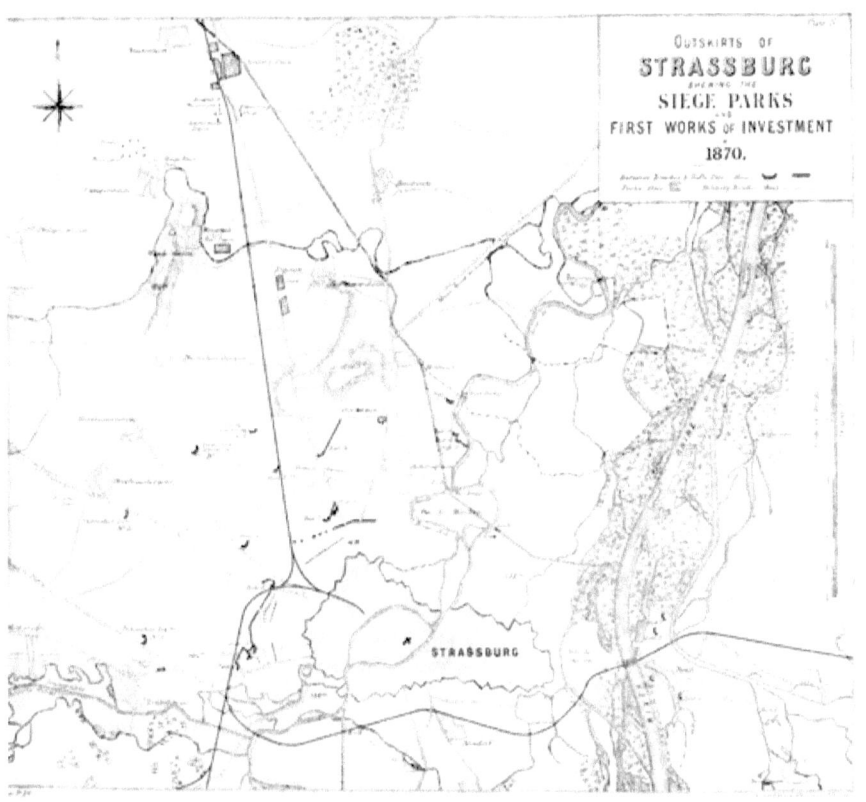

pointed out that, with the increased extent of front of attack, it is no longer possible to have one engineer park; and that the battalions of engineers should each have its own park in its cantonments. The Germans, however, after the widest experience, have decided on having general parks; but, to get over the difficulties, which must occur with a wide front of attack, they provide the different sections with intermediate depôts, and keep them supplied from the park. Of these depôts there are usually three; viz., for the right, centre, and left attacks (as at Strassburg in 1870); they are placed out of sight of the fortress, and distant from it 1,500 to 2,500 yards.[1] These contain the necessary supplies for a "siege day," and from them supplies are issued to moveable *trench depôts*, which are made to progress with the works, and contain supplies for immediate use, laid in the reverse of parallels, &c., often where the approaches join them. With us, each engineer field company has its own equipment, all of which, except perhaps the mining tools, &c., it might retain at its own cantonments; but the siege equipment and stores are, doubtless, most generally available, if placed in a main park, under the control of an officer who, with his staff, is responsible for the entire working of the supplies for siege purposes. Gillmore[2] points out that this park director should be empowered to purchase such stores as he may urgently require; that he should always have the command of a limited number of teams, waggons, &c., to meet sudden calls; and that his books should, at all times, show the state and place of all stores, and particularly of the siege material that is being worked up. By feeding the depôts from the park, they are kept supplied with none but serviceable tools and materials. All tools and stores unfit for use, are passed back at once to the park, where they are dealt with as required.

<small>Intermediate depôts.</small>

<small>Trench depôts.</small>

In the artillery park the arrangement is somewhat <small>Artillery park.</small>

[1] Goetze (p. 174) mentions two such, before Paris, at Meudon and Clamart.
[2] Pp. 237-240.

different, as most of the siege guns are in time, told off to the different siege companies. The reserve, however, as well as the mortars and special pieces, are kept in charge of the park director, who also has charge of—

1st. The artillery siege stores, forges, spare carriages, and moveable platforms.

2nd. The ammunition and laboratory.

3rd. The general powder magazine and the filling and shifting sheds.

From this park are supplied any intermediate depôts of ammunition; while the magazines, and shell recesses in the batteries correspond to the engineer trench depôts.

Importance of completing the railway communications. Presuming, for the reasons already given, that in most large sieges there will be at least one railway, or water communication, approaching the parks; it becomes very desirable to connect them therewith by rails. The line from Balaclava to the trenches before Sebastopol, was the first instance of this being done; though, from want of previous practice and organization, it took eight months to make the $8\frac{3}{4}$ miles. Tiedemann mentions that, at the siege of Longdwy, in 1870, the German engineers reconstructed $4\frac{3}{4}$ miles of railway, from Longuyon to Cons-la-Grandeville, where stood their general siege park; but the largest work of the kind was the field railway between Remilly and Pont-à-Mousson, made in the same war; more, however, for strategical than for siege purposes. The site, which had been examined before the war, was again surveyed on the 14th—16th of August,[1] after which the 22 miles of

---

[1] "About 2,750 were civilians of the country, and, in addition, four companies of engineers and two railway companies, and a park of over 330 carriages. The line was almost all without ballast; the ruling gradient was 1 in 40; the radius of the least curve about 210 yards; while that at Nanteuil was as little as 133 yards. The rails were got from neighbouring lines; the sleepers were cut on the spot or brought up. The works were a few small bridges, and very low cuttings, and embankments of only four or five feet. The engine could only draw four trucks at a time, as the line was very rough for want of ballast. The bridge over the Moselle was carried away after the line was made."
—JACQMIN, pp. 326-328.

line were formed in forty-eight days, by the daily
labour of about 4,000 men. The short line at Nanteuil,
5,450 yards in length, took twenty-one days to complete (pl. ii.).

It generally happens that portions of the line near
the fortress cannot be used for traffic; and from them
rails and other materials may often be obtained to
make the new portion, which should, of course, have
the same gauge, so as to save break of bulk. Any
railway over which waggons can pass, even at low
speed, is better than a road, even if it be too rough
for ordinary engines: in which case, the steam sappers, which have spare railway wheels, may be used
to get the trucks along, one or two at a time, over
steep inclines or weak bridges.[1] Animals, too, may
be worked for the same purpose, and will have a much
greater effective power of draught than on roads.[2]

Use of steam sappers.

Horses, &c.

Only a single line will, generally, be possible; but
it should have a loop, long enough to take the longest
trains, halfway between the main line and park station. At the latter there should be several long
sidings, furnished with a water supply for the engines,
and with swinging derricks, and side and end unloading platforms, these last being required for getting
guns off the waggons. In addition, a telegraph will
be necessary from the main line to the park, with a
station at the loop, so as to work the traffic with the
assistance of signals.

Loop and sidings.

A telegraph and signals required.

[1] Provided, of course, that the gauge be the ordinary English gauge
of 4 ft. 8½ in. Under special circumstances, these engines may be
used as traction engines; but, as a rule, the fuel consumed is out of
proportion to the work done, and exceeds the weight of forage for the
same horse-power. There are four to each army corps.

[2] On the level, with low speeds, the effort of traction, on different
kinds of roads, has been found to be as follows, viz.:

On an unmade track	300 lbs. a ton,	or 1 in 8.
On the best coach roads	45 lbs. ,,	or 1 in 50.
On a plank track	30 lbs. ,,	or 1 in 75.
On a contractor's railway	15 lbs. ,,	or 1 in 150.
On a permanent railway	8 lbs. ,,	or 1 in 280.

The disproportion decreases as the gradient becomes steep, and for
tramways, gradients of from 1 in 30 to 1 in 25, according to their
greater or less length, seem about the steepest practicable. At low
speeds a horse can exert a pull of about 100 lbs.

When it is considered that the distance between the parks and the intermediate depôts may be above two miles, it is plain that a further extension of the railway from the parks to, or towards, those depôts, is very desirable; particularly for the purpose of bringing up the large daily supplies of ammunition that are, as we have already seen, now required.

A railway from the parks to the siege-works.

Having decided to continue the railway, it next becomes a question how best to do so. In the first place, if no trench railway rolling-stock can be brought up, the local gauge must be continued as far as may be: if possible to the intermediate depôts and first artillery position. This arrangement saves break of bulk, but, on the other hand, the width of gauge adds greatly to the labour of construction, and is unsuitable for a further advance along siege approaches, where sharp curves may be unavoidable.

Trench railways.

Next, supposing that narrow-gauge rolling-stock can be brought up, though their weight may hinder the bringing up of special rails; in such case it would, generally, be best to form a narrow-gauge line with the local rails, from the parks onwards. This break of gauge at the parks, is not, except in the case of guns, of great importance: because the demand for rolling-stock between the parks and the base will be so great, and the siding space so comparatively small, that the trucks could seldom be kept loaded at the parks till their contents were wanted at the front.

As, however, the supply of local rails available for trench railways would rarely suffice, and would, generally, be much more clumsy than need be; it will often be worth while to bring up special materials for a narrow-gauge line in advance of the parks; provided that the *difficulties of transport be not excessive*.

For narrow-gauge lines, the points to be considered are:—

Description of rail.

1. The description of rail, if local rails be not used.
2. The width of gauge.
3. The means of locomotion.

If circumstances justify or compel the bringing up of special rails, instead of the use of the local rails, they should be as light as will answer; flat-footed, so as to be fixed without chairs; and of wrought iron, not steel, so as to permit of being easily bent and cut. When timber is plentiful on the spot, very light rails, with numerous broad sleepers, may be used; when not so, heavier rails and fewer sleepers may be better. Rails from 15 to 24 lbs. to the yard will generally be found to answer. One pattern of rail, and one method of fixing should, of course, be used throughout—a lesson that our Abyssinian experience taught us to our cost.

Width of gauge. The width of gauge should be as small as will permit the carriage of the loads, in order to allow of the use of sharp curves, and to diminish the size of the trucks, and also to keep them as much under cover as possible: at the same time it must be wide enough for use with horses. For this, a gauge as narrow as 18 in. has been found practicable; and wide enough for the carriage, at low speeds, of considerable loads.[1]

For reasons that we shall consider further on, we may assume that the siege batteries will seldom be much in advance of the position of the first parallel. It is doubtful, therefore, that it will be worth while to carry a trench railway further, except in short lengths, for mining or other special work.

Means of locomotion. As to the use of railway engines at a siege, it is well known that, besides being incapable of unceasing work, or long-continued effort on steep gradients, horses require a greater weight of forage, for the

---

[1] The trench railway used at Chatham had, at first, a gauge of 2 ft., with rails 15 lbs. to a yard, and with sleepers 2 ft. 6 in. apart. Since then an 18 in. gauge and a 24 lb. rail have been decided on, because this gauge is now in use in England, and plant from it, can be got at need. For this gauge our siege equipment provides, for each army corps—3 engines, 5 trollies, and 25 sets of 18 ft. bogies, as well as 200 tons of rails and 11,000 sleepers, *i. e.*, enough for about 8,000 yards of single line with curves, sidings, &c. The weight of this portion of equipment would be a good deal over 300 tons; while that of a Prussian engineer siege train complete is only about 150 or 160 tons. This might not be a great difficulty when working near a sea base, as at Sebastopol; or provided there be railway communication with the base; but would be entirely beyond the ordinary means of transport, in many inland operations.

work they do even on tramways, than the weight of coals necessary for an engine: it is plain therefore that the latter should be used as far as possible: but an engine, having to move along a definite line, is an easy mark, unless it be so screened that its exact position is uncertain. Hence, except when so screened, it will not be practicable to use engines within the effective range of the fortress artillery, and then not further than the first artillery position. In exceptional cases, as, for instance, on steep gradients, it may be an advantage to use locomotives as stationary engines.[1] In cases where the prolongation of the ordinary line, or the transport of special materials is impracticable; it may still be possible either to form plank tramways, or to provide and make wire tramway lines, such as are used in many mining districts: these seem peculiarly suitable for transporting ammunition; while the materials they are composed of are themselves comparatively light, and easily brought up.

ORGANIZATION OF A PARK.

In addition to the questions of communications and site, the points to be attended to in organizing a park are:—

1st. The adoption of a compact arrangement, which will aid supervision, without crowding the stores.

2nd. The separation and marking of the stores according to their uses, bearing in mind the greater or less frequency of demand.

3rd. The placing of the heavier stores in the positions from whence they can be most easily moved.

4th. The provision of cover for those stores which might be damaged by exposure.

5th. The provision of workshops and hut, shed, and stable accommodation.

6th. The water supply and drainage of the park, and the internal communications.

[1] Handyside's engines, which can be attached to the rails, draw loads up 1 in 10.

Steam Machinery for an Engineer Park

7th. The means of telegraphing to the intermediate depôts, and elsewhere.

8th. The constant employment of the same staff.

9th. The special precautions necessary for securing the park from fire, and the magazines from explosions.[1]

The following subdivision of the site of the engineer park has been found convenient in practice, viz.:— *Engineer park.*

Quarters for the park director and staff, and guard-room for the park guard.

A place for waggons, timber carts, barrows, &c.

Ditto for brushwood work.

Ditto for materials.

Ditto for intrenching tools.

Ditto for sapping tools.

Ditto for mining tools, &c.

Ditto for miscellaneous implements and stores.

Ditto for a magazine for mining powder and for gun-cotton.[1]

Ditto for workshops, saw-pits, sheds for engines, and steam machinery (pl. v.).

Ditto for a canteen.

The same system is followed in the intermediate depôts as far as it is applicable.

PREPARATIONS FOR A SIEGE.

After the assembly of the siege troops on the scene of action, not a little time may elapse before the arrival of the trains; time that may, however, be profitably spent in getting ready for the siege in several ways, in addition to preparing the parks and their communications, and securing defensively any ground wrested from the besieged. In the first place, the resources of the neighbourhood, in the way

---

[1] In the engineer park the wet gun-cotton might be kept in metal-lined powder cases, sunk in the ground; a drying shed might be required to prepare a portion of it for use; but, if possible, enough dry should be kept in store, separate from the wet, the detonators being also kept *apart* from the cotton.

of tools and materials, are collected. Thus Goetze mentions, that at the siege of Paris in 1870, the whole country, as far as Orleans, was requisitioned for nails, wire, &c. The cutting and making up of brushwood also, is at once begun. Brushwood being bulky and troublesome to shift, every care should be taken to avoid moving it more than need be. When the troops may be required to resist sorties at short notice near their cantonments, it may often be best to bring the brushwood to the cantonments, to be made up on the spot; in other cases, to save transport, it may be worked up where cut, particularly when the materials are near the intermediate depôts, to which the gabions and fascines may, in such case, be carried direct.[1] In addition, some brushwood should be stored in the engineer park, to be made up for special purposes, which occur from time to time. In this work of carrying, the German field-artillery teams, the cavalry, and the pontoon trains largely assisted in 1870.

Collection of stores and brushwood.

COMMENCEMENT OF THE SIEGE WORKS.

Besides the brushwood work, those portions of the siege works which are screened from the fortress, within the line of investment, may be at once commenced; the necessary reconnaissances too, must somehow be made. In this respect we have seen, that the besieger is now much hindered by his inability to get near the place; and the only remedy that appears hopeful, is the use of balloon and other observatories.

Balloon observatories.

As, up to the present time, the navigation of balloons has not been effected to any extent, the fortress can only use them as a means of sending out messages, as was done in Paris, and in one or two other places in France, in 1870-71. There is nothing, how-

---

[1] The quantity of brushwood estimated as wanted for a siege, should be exceeded in the preparation, by at least one-fourth.

ever, to prevent an investing force from using the wind, to carry a balloon from one point to another of their line, so as to see into the fortress, and even, as has been suggested, to shell it with gun-cotton. Captive or stationary balloons supply each side with the means, in still weather, of overlooking the works of the other. The French in Paris (1870-71) used a captive balloon in this way, and, by its means, discovered that the Germans were employed on the defences of Pierrefitte. The observer signalled to Fort la Briche, which opened at 3,000 metres, and stopped the infantry working parties. The gas balloons they used in that siege had a capacity of about 20,000 cubic feet, and carried three men. At Strassburg and Paris, in 1870-71, a stationary balloon was tried for the Germans, by an American, but without success. At Aldershot, in 1863, a captive balloon made ten or twelve ascents to a height of 1,100 or 1,200 feet, and was found quite manageable in still weather. For the purpose of observing at a siege, as the field of operations is limited, only a small ascent of from 300 to 600 feet is necessary. The balloon is best secured by a light steel wire rope, and two silk or hemp ropes, as in fig. 15.[1] It must have buoyancy enough to sustain an observer, in telegraphic communication with the earth, and an aeronaut. This is not difficult to arrange in a great fortress, where coal gas can be got;[2] but, though gas works may sometimes be found by the besieger, in the towns he occupies near the

[1] The insulation of this steel rope might be so arranged, that it would act as a telegraphic conductor, instead of using a separate wire. Besides, it seems best to use at least one metal rope, as all others wear quickly, and may rot without showing it. 800 feet of ⅜-in. steel rope (of fine wires for suppleness) would weigh 70 lbs., and have a breaking resistance of 1 ton. 1,600 feet of 1¼-in. silk rope would weigh 129 lbs. and be of the same strength.

[2] In considering the use of coal gas, it is to be remembered that at certain stages of production, a much lighter, and therefore more suitable gas is obtained, than at others.

The French war balloon, taken to Italy in 1859, was filled with coal gas at Milan, and brought *filled* to Gorgonzola, twenty miles off. It held 30,000 cubic feet.

fortress, whence the filled balloon can be led to the point of ascent; the contrary will often be the case. Monsieur Godard proposes to have four small balloons of manageable size for each captive balloon; and to fill and bring up these to the latter. When, however, the distance is great, it may be practicable and, in certain cases, with a sea base for instance, more convenient, to bring up compressed gas for the besiegers' use. Coal gas can be compressed to one-fortieth of its bulk, by means of an engine of three or four horse-power; in this way the gas required for a balloon, say 16,000 cubic feet, could be reduced to 400 cubic feet; the chief difficulty would be the weight of the reservoirs, which, even if of steel, would probably weigh altogether about seven or eight tons, and would require two railway trucks for their transport. Hydrogen gas can be compressed to the same extent, and, being more buoyant,[1] about 13,000 to 14,000 cubic feet would answer the purpose, particularly as the buoyancy of pure hydrogen, such as could be brought up, is nearly 70 lbs., while that of light coal gas is only 50 lbs. per 1,000 cubic feet.

Compressed gas for balloons.

Local means of inflating balloons.

Supposing, however, that there are no means on the spot for making coal gas, and that we cannot bring up compressed gas; we must seek for local means of inflating balloons, for siege and field operations. Hydrogen gas, the smoke of straw or wool, and hot air are the means that have been, so far, used with any success. The production of the first, in large quantities, requires time and heavy apparatus; and yet the armies of the first French Republic made large use of hydrogen captive balloons, particularly at the battle of Fleurus and at the siege of Ehrenbreitstein; and even shifted a filled one from Charleroy to Maubeuge. The method that has been

---

[1] The buoyancy of 1,000 feet of hydrogen, as made in the field, is roughly 62·5 lbs.; and of common coal gas about 45 lbs., or in the proportion of 12·5 to 9.

The weight of a balloon with ballast for a small ascent, and with telegraph and cables, should be under 800 or 900 lbs., including two men. A surplus buoyancy of 10 to 20 lbs. being enough to start the ascent.

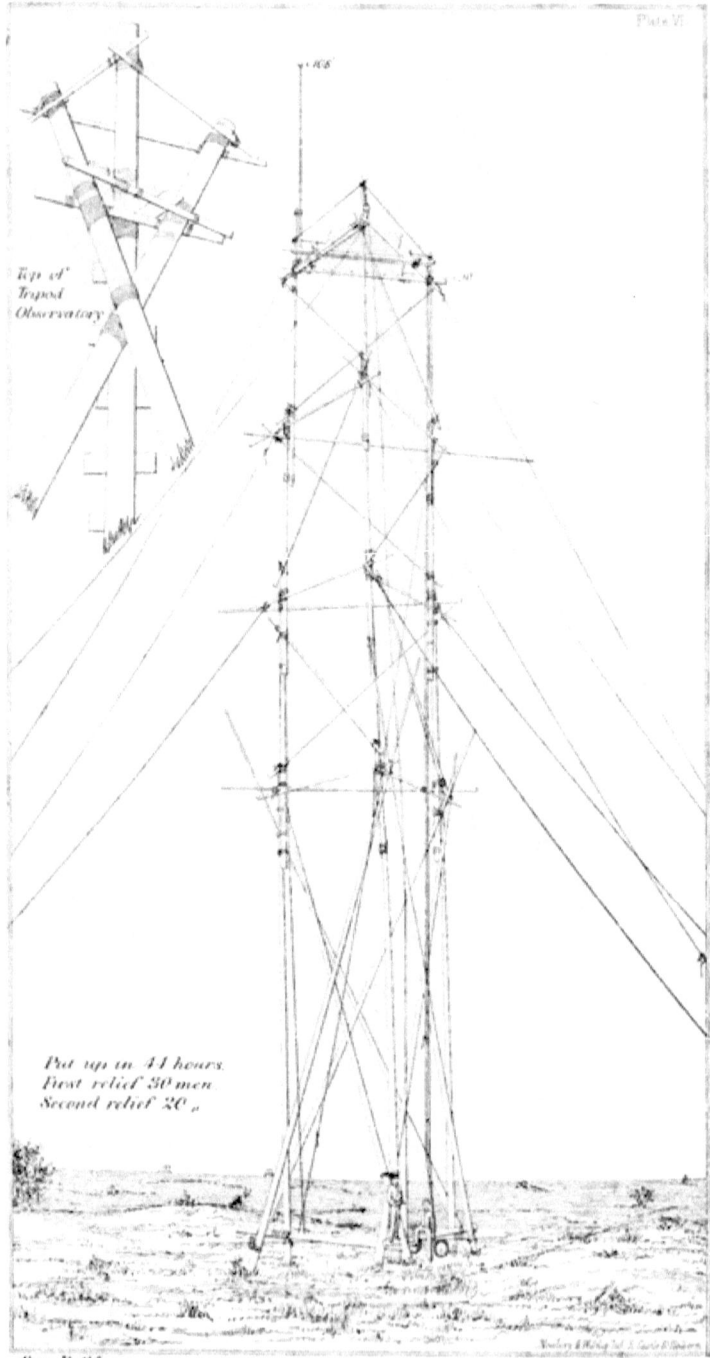

found to answer best for making hydrogen, seems to be to pass steam over red-hot iron or zinc. The American balloons used in 1862-3, were inflated with hydrogen, prepared in three or four hours by the sulphuric acid process, and were much used with M'Clellan's army.[1] The production of hydrogen is, therefore, possible at a siege; but, apart from the difficulty of making it, there is another point against its use, namely, the great diffusive power of the gas, which makes the choice of the fabric for the balloon especially difficult. The employment of a double balloon may, however, prove to be a remedy.

Of the other two modes of inflation, hot air seems to promise best;[2] and it is proposed that the balloon be inflated, in the first instance, by any convenient number of sources of heat, and the air be kept hot, during the ascent, by a very powerful lamp, burning vegetable oil. Even supposing, however, that a balloon is available, its use is so dependent on weather, &c., that more reliable methods of observation must also be employed.

Hot-air balloons.

Other observatories are of two kinds:—

1st. Those which are beyond the effective fire of the defender, and depend for their use on the height to which they are raised.

2nd. Those which are chiefly valuable from their position, and which may be exposed to fire.

Other observatories.

Elevated observatories.

To equip the first, the R.E. siege train should have a few very powerful telescopes. This kind may be placed on existing objects, churches, trees, &c., or may be built up of timber (pl. vi). Observatories of this class, some of them over 140 feet high, were used at the siege of Charleston.[3] They were protected at the base by a defensible stockade.

One of the best forms for the field is the ladder-tripod.[4] This constitutes a portable observatory,

---

[1] P. P. R. E., vol. xii., papers x. to xii.

[2] The buoyancy of white smoke is about 22.5 lbs. to 1,000 cubic feet; hence Montgolfier balloons must be very large; but they are inflated in half an hour. A captive Montgolfier balloon was used for the French at Solferino in 1859.

[3] Gillmore, p. 291.   [4] P. P. R. E., vol. vii., p. 45.

which can be raised in twenty minutes to a height of forty feet.

Concealed observatories.

The second kind, usually take the form of blindages, with shell-proof roofs if exposed; or they may be concealed behind any convenient objects. In all cases they should have telegraphic communication with the rear, and the same two observers should always take alternative reliefs.[1]

Siege telegraphy.

While discussing these collateral questions, it will not be out of place to consider the subject of telegraphy as applied to siege purposes. The lines of telegraph employed are of three kinds:—

1st. Those for connecting the head-quarters with the base of operations.

2nd. Those for communicating along the line of investment.

3rd. Those for connecting the different operations of the siege itself.

For the first kind the line will be semi-permanent, and ordinary telegraphic materials will be used.[2]

For the second, the arrangements will be similar to those made in the case of an ordinary defensive position, for which the eighteen miles of wire with the telegraph half-troop attached to each army corps, is sufficient.

For the third, the lines must be so arranged as to give the siege troops the means of calling for help, as soon as they are threatened by a great sortie; to enable the siege batteries to work collectively, by carrying a branch wire to some point situated centrally with reference to each group of batteries; and also, by carrying forward the telegraph from the siege head-quarters, to the quarters of the staff for the day, and from thence into some blinded observatories in the advanced trenches. From these points, the effects of the artillery fire, the earliest notice of a sortie, or the evacuation of a work, may, at once, be reported, and thus immediate action when needful

---

[1] P. P. R. E., vol. xx., pl. xxxii., fig. 34.

[2] According to the "Regulations for the Supply of Stores to an Army in the Field," our reserve telegraph equipment is to be 100 miles of double line of bare wire, with 10 stations.

may be secured; or, on the other hand, the siege troops may be saved from unnecessary alarms, or enabled to communicate with the parks for supplies.

For these purposes, our siege equipment provides eighteen miles of galvanized bare wire, and eighteen miles of insulated wire. The former would be used to connect the siege head-quarters with those of the head-quarter staff, and also for such portions of the line from the siege head-quarters to the advanced works, as are not much exposed, and where an aerial line is admissible; beyond this the insulated wire is laid, if possible, on, or when absolutely necessary, under the ground, in rear of the trenches and approaches. If deeply buried, it is hard to find out and repair faults, &c.

The failure of an aerial line, as compared with a ground one, was shown at Paris in 1870, when the French had a double system, connecting the forts and advanced works with head-quarters. A few days' firing so disabled the aerial line, that the attempt to maintain it was abandoned.

In the Crimea we used about eighteen miles of telegraph, with seven or eight stations, the chief ones being at Balaclava, the head-quarters, and the engineer park of the left attack. The line was buried eighteen inches under ground. The Americans, in 1863, brought their lines as far as the second parallel before Fort Wagner; and we learn from Tiedemann that, at Strassburg, in 1870, the Germans carried the field telegraph as far as the third parallel, whence, by means of a captured countermine gallery, they observed and telegraphed back the effects of the curved fire against a scarp of lunette 53. Before Paris, at the head-quarters of the invader, military telegraphy received its largest development (pl. i.); and at the second siege, the assailants carried their telegraph into the advanced trenches, before the Point du Jour, whence the fire of the advanced batteries, and of those at Montretout, was regulated by observation, and that of the latter stopped as the troops entered.

As an addition to the telegraph, or as a substitute

for it, visual signals may be usefully employed at a siege; in the daytime by means of flags, and at night, by hand-lamps and lime-lights. Of the latter, 36 are provided in our siege equipment for each army corps.[1]

Electric lights, to illuminate the ground over which night attacks may advance, are likely to form part of the siege equipment; and they may, in such case, be available also for signalling; but, hitherto, they have not effected much in the way of illumination; and as the machinery[2] for each light weighs nearly a ton, and requires an engine of 6 horse-power, their use is more within the power of the defence, than the attack. In any case there is nothing to show that the latter is likely either to gain or suffer much by their use at ranges exceeding 800 to 1,200 yards in favourable weather, and at less ranges in mist or fog; though their employment by the defence, in the latter stages of its resistance, in combination with light balls, rockets, and parachute lights, will, not a little, increase the difficulties of the assailants.

COMPOSITION OF THE SIEGE TRAINS.

Before discussing the ends to be attained by the different siege works, we have to consider the material means, viz., the artillery and engineer siege

---

[1] "At Sebastopol, the Russians employed Cossacks with flags to regulate their indirect fire against bodies of the allied troops; while at the siege of Belfort in 1870, the Germans arranged a system of signals with flags and with the electric light. Visual signals were largely used in the same war by the Second German Army Corps before Paris."—GOETZE.

[2] The Gramme and Siemens dynamo-electric machines promise best at present. The intensity of the ray can be somewhat increased by diminishing its spread; but, to secure searching power, a horizontal spread of 15 degrees and a vertical spread of 5 degrees seem desirable. The observing or shooting parties should be placed well to one flank of the light, which should be capable of being shifted. The electric light due to a large Groves' battery, which is more portable than the steam arrangement, will show troops at night at a distance of 500 yards.

trains. On the complete organization and provision of these, depend, in great measure, the quickness with which the assailant can strike the defender at a disadvantage. To what we lost in the Crimea for want of this, we need not refer; but even in 1870, the preparations for the siege of Strassburg, were so retarded, as to cause no little delay in beginning.[1]

The strength of a siege train for any one operation, should depend on the circumstances of the case; and the artillery train should, by way of providing for contingencies,[2] have 10 or 15 per cent. more guns than can be employed at any one time. In most countries it is customary to decide on a unit of siege train, several of which go to form the train; the unit itself being composed of the different natures, in the proportions thought best. At present we have a *heavy* and a *light* siege train unit, the former to consist of eight 64-pounders, eight 40-pounders, and fourteen 8-in. rifled howitzers; the latter, of ten 40-pounders, ten 6·3-inch rifled howitzers, and ten 25-pounders, all M.L.R. The arrangement is convenient for small sieges, where only the lighter guns would be wanted; but for large operations, all the natures would be required; and in considering the proportions, we shall assume that the two units are combined. These proportions depend on the different functions the guns have to perform, viz.:—

Artillery siege train.

1st. To repel sorties.

2nd. By means of direct fire, to bombard distant works; to dismount guns; to pierce and cut down traverses; to enfilade unprotected lines; and, occasionally, to destroy iron-plated defences.

3rd. By means of curved or high angle fire, to search out the interiors of works; to enfilade the parts provided with traverses; to demolish blindages, magazines, and parados; and to breach escarps, caponieres, &c.

4th. In the advanced stages of the attack, to keep

[1] "Revue d'Artillerie," viii., p. 386.
[2] Wolff mentions (pp. 408-411) that 55 German guns and 7 carriages broke down after an average of 800 to 1,300 rounds; but the French fire disabled many more carriages than guns.

down the fire of the place, so as to permit of the progress of the near approaches.

5th. In the close attack, to impede the defence by a continuous hail of shells dropped into the works.

6. To batter flank defences, revetments, keeps, and retrenchments at close quarters; and to arm lodgments in captured works.

Guns for defence.

For the first purpose, in addition to the field artillery, which will answer in most cases, a proportion of guns of the class of our 25-pounder M.L.R. is required; so as to secure a preponderance over any field batteries that may accompany a sortie. For this, too, the 64-pounder howitzer may, in some cases, be employed; as, for instance, against villages. A proportion of Gatling guns, which, in certain special cases, are valuable for the defence of positions, are also likely to be used.[1] Gatling guns can be aimed with accuracy, in given directions, at night; an advantage that the small arm does not possess: this gives them superiority over musketry fire against attacks in the dark.[2]

Guns for direct fire.

For the second purpose, considerable range, great accuracy, comparatively flat trajectory, and high velocity to secure great striking power are the important points. In most European siege trains, the favourite gun for this purpose seems to be the long 15-c. B.L.R. gun. The guns in our service, which most nearly correspond with this, are the 64-pounder M.L.R. of 64 cwt., and the 40-pounder M.L.R., the one rather a heavier, and the other rather a lighter, gun. Under this head we have to consider a more

---

[1] "Thus the Bavarians used their mitrailleurs, for the defence of their part of the line of investment before Paris in 1870-71."—GOETZE.

[2] The full value of Gatling guns will not be felt until they are made more *portable* than the lightest cannon; less *complicated* than at present; and capable of firing the *small arm cartridges*. The weight of the small service Gatling is more than twice that of a gun firing an 11-lb. shell; and too much is sacrificed to automatic action and quick firing. A Gatling gun of half the weight, mounted on light bicycle wheels, and really moveable by hand, would, surely, be a more useful weapon, even if it fired only half as fast as the present one, tied, as it is, to a heavy gun-carriage and weighing altogether over a ton.

powerful class of gun, not included in our siege train, but which, either our necessities, or opportunities, may lead us to use. Although land fortresses are not rich in iron defences, we may, particularly in operations on the coast, have to deal with armour-plated works.[1] Against very light plating, we might employ the 64-pounder of the siege train, with its excellent battering shell of 90 lbs.; and when this would be insufficient, we might, now and then, bring up the 7-in. gun of 90 cwt., adapted for siege purposes; or else draw on the navy for their 7-in. and 8-in. guns, which pierce about 9 and 9½ inches of iron. These we should bring into battery on rails if possible; though, even without such aids, the Americans, in 1863, brought 11·5-ton guns into battery before Charleston under very difficult conditions. As there is no need to resort to guns of this weight for high angle or vertical fire, because rifled howitzers, throwing as large shells, are much more portable;[2] we may assume that they will rarely be used, except for the work that they alone can do, namely, the destruction of armour or of very massive masonry. Hence, their object being defined, they will require but little training; their fire, however, must be direct, and their range short, say 1,000 to 1,500 yards, a fact that further restricts their use.

For the third purpose the qualifications are, a small limit of error at long ranges and very high angles, and at shorter ranges, with angles of elevation less than 20°, a uniform trajectory, extreme accuracy, and considerable final velocity. In our service, the pieces we should expect to see used for the purpose, are the 8-in. and 6·3-in. R. howitzers: of the capabilities of the latter it would be premature to speak, but, should it not prove efficient in these

Guns for curved fire.

---

[1] Metz is being provided with a few turrets, plated with about 6 inches of iron. Antwerp has also some iron defences. At short ranges, the battering shell of our 64-pounder would pierce 6 inches of iron; and repeated blows would destroy even a greater thickness.

[2] Thus the 10-in. R. howitzer of 6 tons, throws a shell of 350 lbs.; while the Palliser shell of the 8-in. gun of 9 tons weighs only 181·5 lbs.: the same almost as that of the 8-in. howitzer of 46 cwt.

respects, it is not too much to say that our train will be wanting in one very important and necessary element. On the Continent the gun most commonly used is the short 15-c. B.L. gun, the excellent qualities of which, have been fully tested, both by experiment and in the war of 1870-71. This gun can be fired with a shell of 2½ calibres, and also with the shell of the long 15-c. gun: an advantage not possessed by M.L. guns of the same bore, but with a different twist, on account of the difference in the positions of the studs.[1] The 21-c. B.L. mortar, which is fired from a bed, not a carriage, is also much used on the Continent, and corresponds in calibre with our 8-inch howitzer; though the latter is more of a shell-gun than a mortar. It is chiefly used for firing at high angles, against the roofs of casemates, &c., when great penetration is required, and for breaching. To supplement guns of this class, 8 in. and 10-in. smooth-bore mortars may also be used.

Light trench guns.

For the fourth purpose extreme mobility, flat trajectory, and a moderate destructive power are the qualities required. Future experience may show that the heavy Gatling guns of 0·65-in. bore, such as are adopted in Russia, are suitable; but, in the absence of experience, we incline to the belief that very light shell-guns (as light even as the 7-pounder or 9-pounder M.L.R. guns, so as to have extreme mobility) will, combined with the use of portable Gatlings and wall pieces prove most effective. To these guns we shall have occasion to refer further on; but on the subject of wall pieces we may remark that, having a mobility not much inferior to that of a small arm, they can be used when nothing on wheels can be employed. They can be shifted from place to place, almost as quickly as, and attract no more attention than, a musket. At the same time, the weapon being "nobody's child," has, except in Prussia, almost dropped out of use. The artillery make it, and bring it up with their trains; the infantry shoot with it, but do not like the clumsy thing; while the engineers,

Wall pieces.

[1] The use of a gas check, however, now promises to do away with the necessity for studs.

who never handle it, derive the most benefit from its use. Hence, though its value is not denied, and its introduction has been urged by soldiers of great experience;[1] it is plain that, useful as it is, nothing but the exercise of the highest authority can bring it into the service. Of its use we have not a little evidence from the war of 1870-71. The most remarkable feature of the siege of Strassburg, was the way in which the light 9-c. siege guns, on high carriages, and the wall pieces in the hands of infantry detachments, *completely silenced* the fire of the place. At Belfort too, wall pieces were used in the attack of the " Perches," though with less marked success. They also formed part of the artillery siege train brought up against Paris.[2]

The best argument in their favour is, however, the fact that, in the new Prussian siege train, the proportion of wall pieces to guns and mortars is as three to eight.[3]

The conditions that a wall piece has to fulfil are:— *Conditions.*

1st. To have a greater penetration, and a somewhat greater effective range than the small arm.

2nd. To be fit to fire from the shoulder without a stand, when rested, as it would be, on a bank or parapet.

3rd. To be handy, and easily moved and loaded.

[1] Cf. " The Military Opinions of Sir J. Burgoyne," p. 304.

[2] Goetze (p. 186) mentions that they enabled the Germans to drive the French out of part of Les Moulineaux, south of Paris.

[3] The present pattern of German wall piece, which is about to be improved, and adapted for a solid cartridge, is a B.L. on the Zündnadel-gewehr principle; barrel cast steel; length, 39·44 in.; bore, 0·928 in.; twist, one complete turn in the length; bullet, cast iron or steel, 2·08 in. long, weight, 3 oz.; charge, 0·75 oz.; weight of piece, 62 lbs. These pierce a gabion filled with earth, and go through two feet of sand-bag parapet at 250 to 300 paces: the bullets often break up. The wall pieces we took at Bomarsund, in 1854, were B.L. pieces weighing 23·5 lbs.; length of barrel, 42·5 in.; weight of conical bullets, 4 oz.; diameter of bore, 0·875 in.; they were fitted with a swivel pin intended for a socket. The Austrian B.L. wall piece, weighing 15 lbs., is effective up to 1,300 yards; it is furnished with a tripod; and its bullet weighs 3·3 oz.—*See* " *Revue d'Artillerie,*" July, 1874.

For the first, Sir John Burgoyne suggested a penetration, greater than that of the small arm by one-third or a quarter. In any case mobility should be the first consideration, when a penetration double that of the musket is secured. The requirements for penetration are, a high velocity, and a hard tough bullet of the greatest weight that the shoulder will stand.[1] The size, and weight of the piece, will insure a somewhat greater effective range than that of the musket, and experiment may show that telescopic sights would be a gain; as, even with small bores, the Confederates used telescopes with success at Charleston.[2]

For the second, the recoil must be such as a man can stand. Hence a very light gun is not likely to answer. There are several ways of diminishing the recoil, for instance, the employment of india-rubber or spring-heel plates; the use of an unenlarged chamber; and the removal of the rifling for some distance from the chamber: but even with these, it does not seem likely, that a bullet of over three or four ounces will be convenient.[3] If a stand, or tripod, have to be used, the piece is unfit for shallow rifle pits or other low cover, and wants more space, and is less mobile than without one. At the same time, a ball-joint with a spike to be stuck into the earth might, if fixed to the piece, help to check recoil, and would not be in the way.

For the third, the weight of the piece must not be too heavy for a man to carry, *i.e.*, should not, if possible, exceed 30 and in no case 50 lbs. The

---

[1] The experiments of Whitworth have shown that, for hard bullets, a mild powder is preferable. With hardened steel bullets (fig. 19) of 472 grains and 85 grains of powder, he pierced ½-in. wrought iron plates at angles of 45 degs.: a fact that suggests the advantage of having, for siege purposes, a proportion of steel-headed bullets for the small arm, to be employed against the bullet-proof shields of ¼-in. steel, which will now be so much used. With hard metal bullets, the twist can be given by a gas check.

[2] Gillmore, p. 139.

[3] As by the Declaration of 1868, the smallest explosive bullet must exceed about 14 oz. (400 grammes); the wall-piece bullet, in Europe, at least, must be non-explosive.

barrel should not be extremely long, and should be breech-loading, with a simple side or top action.

We next consider the fifth class of ordnance, between which, and the others there is this difference, that, while these latter are chiefly employed against the defences, and, in most cases, depend for their effect on their penetration before bursting; those of the fifth class, are employed against the defenders, and their bursting effect is diminished by their penetration. While, therefore, they must be handy and easily moved about; what they have to do is, to throw shells, with large bursters, for a few hundred yards, at high angles, and with just enough velocity to secure fair accuracy. Hence it is for the artillery to consider whether a light rifled mortar will, or will not fulfil these conditions better than small wrought iron or steel S.B. mortars of the same weight.[1] The existing 7-pounder, throwing an 11-lb. double shell, is to be thus used on a light mortar-bed. It is so light, it can be shifted by hand. *Pieces to produce surface effect.* *Light rifled mortars.*

If, on this subject, we may venture beyond the limit of what is, we imagine that one form of the mortar of the future, will be a piece in which extreme lightness is secured, by designing it to be fired with the lowest charge which will just carry a very large shell (perhaps of wrought iron) at most 300 or 400 yards, and with the lowest practicable velocity. Under such conditions the weight might surely be small, when we remember that Mallet's built-up mortar threw a shell of 2,660 lbs. a distance of 2,700 yards. *Large portable mortars.*

For the sixth class, guns such as the 25-pounder M.L.R., or the 9 and 12-c. B.L.R. are suitable, and can, if required, be used for breaching, by employing high charges and expending more ammunition. *Guns for close quarters.*

An examination of the lists[2] of the siege trains of those Powers which have reorganized their trains *Comparison of British and foreign siege artillery.*

---

[1] A method of weighting the bed with shells, &c., might permit of greater lightness for transport. The 7-pounder bed weighs 200 lbs., and permits of an elevation of 22 degs.

[2] See Appendix A.

since the war of 1870-71, will show where we differ from continental nations:—

1st. On the whole the weight of our guns is rather above the average, while that of the two natures of short shell guns is a good deal below the average.

2nd. The number of guns in our train requiring separate shells, presuming we must add some light gun for the trenches, is the largest in any train.

3rd. As to the proportions, we seem to carry many more 8-in. howitzers than are found in the other trains; and, assuming that in spite of its light weight, the 6·3-in. howitzer will correspond in efficiency with the short 15-c. gun, we have to notice, that our proportion of them is only about *half* the mean number of the latter, carried in the other trains; considering the number and variety of uses to which this gun can be put, as well as the purposes for which it is peculiarly adapted, the difference is one that deserves attention. On the other hand, we have somewhat more than the average of the corresponding heavy gun. The proportion of 40-pounders is also rather large; however, the gun is so good, and the advantage of using light ammunition, as long as it answers, is so great, that a much smaller number would not perhaps be advisable. The proportion of 25-pounders in our train, which seems rather large, might, perhaps, be diminished in favour of the light 64-pounder.

Gun carriages. Whatever the guns may be, the question of the siege carriage is now of the first importance. Owing to the great increase in range and destructive effect of the shells now fired, with the further increase of accuracy which we may now look for, on both sides, owing to the use of range-finders, and, possibly, to the introduction of telescopic sights: the necessity for increased cover for the detachments, in batteries exposed *Disappearing carriages.* to fire, has become much greater. Plainly, the best way to secure this, is to let the gun recoil under cover; and much ingenuity has been spent in applying counterweights, springs, and hydraulic and pneumatic machinery to store up the work of recoil, so as to raise the gun into the firing position, when loaded.' The first method appears too cumbersome for a siege gun; the second has not succeeded; and the hydro-pneumatic carriage for a 64-pounder, which rises 3 ft. 4 in., and fires over 7 ft. 3 in., adds 56 per cent. to the weight of the carriage: this carriage, though it stood a severe firing test with success, has not been tested by the rough usage of war. At the same time, seeing that it is only by the adoption of a *disappearing* carriage that the attack can be sure of using direct fire at short ranges: it seems certain that future siege trains will be supplied with, at least, a few such carriages. One other plan seems applicable to the very light guns which are so valuable in the advanced trenches. This is, to raise the gun (figs. 17 and 21, pl. xix.) into the firing position *by hand*.[2]

[1] In the "Memoirs of Marshal Saxe," already quoted, there is a picture of a pair of guns worked by tackles, on the twin principle, on inclined planes. A somewhat similar plan was used with great success, by the defenders, at the last siege of Antwerp. The history of most of the modern inventions of this kind is given by King.

[2] The gun can, if not exposed, be kept up for several rounds by clamping the arc; and when necessary, it can be lowered by hand; or if required to recoil under cover, the recoil can be checked by regulating the friction, the gun descending on to side buffers. In such case the carriage must be secured to an anchor in front, to prevent the tendency of the system to rear up; a spiral spring or some such means being used to break the shock on the fastenings. By this method the 7-pounder of 200 lbs. could be raised by two men exerting each a force of 60 to 80 lbs. The 9-pounder of 6 cwt. could be raised by 4 men using a pair of handspikes, as in fig. 18.

Another plan, applicable to mitrailleuses which have no recoil, and that may prove practicable with very light guns, is to have a cranked axle (fig. 21) supporting the carriage, which would rest on bearings in which the axle can turn, means being provided for keying the axle both to the naves and also to the carriage body. For travelling, the crank being lowered, it would revolve as usual in the pipe-boxes, but would be keyed to the carriage; while, for firing, it would be keyed to the naves, if intended to recoil under cover. The recoil would be more than half the circumference of the wheel, and the piece would be raised by manning the wheels and running up; the effort being the same as for running up a corresponding inclined plane, but with the advantage of allowing the gun to be placed in the lowered position, close to the parapet, for shelter when required. For a mitrailleur

High siege carriages.

As soon as we get to guns of position, or of a heavier nature, this method is inapplicable, and, so far, the best solution seems to be the German one (figs. 23, pl. xx. and pl. vii.), of firing from a high carriage. Their high carriages, firing over a 5 ft. 3 in. parapet, were employed throughout the war of 1870-71. These were used up to ranges of 8,300 yards, and with over 30 degs. of elevation; and some of them, as, for instance, those used east of Paris, went through three sieges; while of those at Belfort, only seven broke down. The principle cannot, therefore, be said to be untried in war, and, it may be added, is being generally adopted on the Continent; the Austrian siege carriage, for instance, fires over 5 ft. 9 in.

The application of hydraulic jacks to the carriages will probably obviate the inconvenience felt in 1870, of having to use a gin to lift the guns into the trunnion holes; and, except in cases where direct fire and battering charges are required, the recoil is not likely to cause much difficulty. This method of mounting has the advantage of not requiring deep embrasures.

Disadvantages of embrasures.

The disadvantages of deep embrasures are:—

1st. They offer distinct targets to the enemy, and are easily destroyed by shells.

2nd. They diminish the lateral range of the guns.

3rd. They weaken the parapets, and so diminish the cover they give.

4th. They are constantly blown down by the explosion of their own guns, and check the escape of smoke.

5th. They are troublesome to construct, and difficult to repair.

the axle would be keyed both to naves and carriage while firing, and unkeyed when it required to be lowered under cover.

In order to go forward along narrow trenches, the track of these carriages should be as small as is consistent with stability; and at the spots where it is meant to fire, the trench should be widened and the terreplein raised if necessary.

Should disappearing carriages prove too complicated for these trench guns, as the trenches are likely to be too deep for common carriages, the alternative (fig. 24) will be to place them in rear of the parallel: by means of the ramps, the guns could be constantly shifted, the parallel in front acting as a screen.

Pl. VII

Battery 30, Strassburg, 1870—71.

The first of these facts was proved by our experience and that of the Russians in the Crimea in 1854-55. Todleben, in his account of the defence, mentions that on the 17th of June the allied fire destroyed 200 of his embrasures. In the war of 1870-71 the French found great difficulty with many of their embrasures, which were destroyed by guns they could not reply to. Thus, at Belfort, they had 16 per cent. of their pieces, and 32 per cent. of their carriages disabled; while their fire only destroyed two German guns and seven carriages.[1] During the second siege of Paris, they cut embrasures in the German battery No. vii. at Chatillon: the use to which the battery was put, was, in each case, identical, namely, to counterbatter Fort Issy, which lay 60 metres below;[2] and the Communists there caused the French much greater losses than they had inflicted on the Germans; while, as regards defence, the embrasures of their works were everywhere completely wrecked. After the second siege, while the parapets of the enceinte of Paris were but little injured, and the excellent blindages mostly intact, the guns in embrasures were reduced to the state of lumps of metal in a heap of splinters.

The diminution of lateral range due to embrasures often prevents the use of the siege guns for resisting sorties, and necessitates the making of otherwise unnecessary batteries. Even when embrasures are made with small splay, the parapets are weakened for several feet on each side of the throat; and the part so weakened gives little or no protection, so that, against fire directed on the embrasure, the gun is as much exposed, as in the overbank arrangement, and the detachment more so. The blast of explosion alone, in time, destroys embrasures, and their revetment is apt to take fire. Officers, who were in Fort Issy in 1870, mentioned that they had every night to keep strong working parties engaged at making good their own damages: at Montrouge two hundred men were often employed for this purpose in a night. Lastly,

[1] Wolff, pp. 408-411.
[2] P. P. R. E., vol. xx., p. 22.

embrasures complicate and *delay* the construction of a battery, in which, whether there be embrasures or not, the same relief is necessary: they also require extra materials.[1]

<small>Their disuse.</small>
It is true that, though the embrasures may be shut up, still the parapets between them protect the guns from oblique fire: but, admitting that it is more important for guns to be *able to fire*, than to be *safe from fire*, it appears a necessity that siege carriages, while kept, as regards their height, within the limits of stability, should, for the future, be such as to allow guns to fire overbank when directly opposed to the defensive artillery. In such cases, except with disappearing carriages, shallow unrevetted embrasures with a counterslope will be used; the extra exposure of the guns to enfilade being guarded against by choosing *suitable* positions for the batteries, or by high screens or traverses. Deep embrasures, in spite of their defects, may still be desirable in special cases, those, for instance, in which guns are exposed to a cross-fire alone; or where they are only exposed to indirect fire. In these cases, raised masses between the guns give some protection.

<small>Transport of guns.</small>
A collateral question, important in its bearing on the length and bulk of the train, and on the number of teams it requires is, whether the heavier guns should have separate travelling and fighting carriages. The whole of the guns in the German siege train, as well as our own, travel on the firing carriages. The arrangement is convenient; but it appears a question whether, on the whole, weight would not be saved, and recoil rendered more manageable, in the case of the heaviest guns (the 64 pr. and 8-in. howitzer), by using sliding carriages and

---

[1] Were further evidence wanted, the late Russian experiments supply it.

Guns were fired at, at 1,160 yards, and were mounted as follows:—
    1st, so as to fire through a deep embrasure.
    2nd, so as to fire exposed "overbank."
    3rd, so as to fire "overbank," through shallow embrasures.

To dismount them, the number of shots required were; for the first, 10; for the second, 26; for the third, an average of 63 to 64.—*Revue d'Artillerie*, January, 1877, pp. 343-4.

naval slides or directing bars; rather than fire such heavy pieces off carriages with wheels and axles.

Next to the question of the carriages comes that of the ammunition. A reference to the table will show that the average weight of our siege shells is very high, owing chiefly to the large proportion of 8-in. rifled howitzers. This is, doubtless, an advantage if we can get up the shells; but it throws a considerable strain on our transport. As to the number of rounds to be kept in peace time; seeing that our manufacturing power at least equals that of the rest of Europe, the proportion laid down, viz. 500 rounds, ought to be enough. It should be understood, however, that, for war, a larger number will be required. Hohenlohe tells us that in 1870-71 the reserve store of shells in the park before Paris, varied from 300 to 500 rounds per gun; while 1,000 rounds were thought necessary for the siege.[1] At any rate, the siege cannot be commenced without having 400 or 500 rounds per gun on the spot, with a certainty of the supply being kept up; the total supply being, according to Brunner, about 1,500 rounds for each gun; 600 to 800 for heavy, and 1,200 for light mortars.

As to the number of rounds a day, Hohenlohe states that 50 or 60 per gun was not often exceeded. As a rule, the Germans seldom fired over eight rounds during any single hour in daylight, generally not more than three or four, and fewer at night; as they found, no doubt, that to shoot *straight*, one must shoot *steady;* and, further, they had to *nurse* their breech-loaders, which cannot be fired continuously at the same rate as muzzle-loaders; besides which, the firing is now much more regulated by observation, which involves delay.

The *quantity* of ammunition, too, that can be spared for each day, has become a more serious question. In certain cases, where time does not press, and construction is easy, magazines for two or three days' supply may be made, if the site be a secure

---

[1] Gœtze.

one: but, as a rule, room for a supply for twenty-four hours can, alone, be allowed. At the first batteries, where the making and supply of magazines is easy, there should be room for 160 rounds; the greatest number required being, probably, 72 rounds for the first six or seven hours, and the same for the remainder of the twenty-four. Breaching batteries, for direct fire, might, possibly, require the same accommodation: while those for curved fire would use, at most, 8 rounds for each hour of the day, and 3 at night: for these, 140 rounds might be provided. For other purposes a smaller supply would suffice. It seems reasonable, therefore, to reckon on having to provide for not more than 100 to 160 rounds per gun, for twenty-four hours' supply, in the battery magazines. This will lessen the size of the magazines, which we have, for some years past, been making for 380 rounds per gun; or for 20 per hour in the day, and for 10 per hour in the night.

Composition of engineer siege train. The composition of the engineer siege train is based on the gun unit, which was, till lately, one of thirty-five guns. It may now be necessary that the train should be composed, with reference both to the light and to the double unit, supposing the latter to be employed for large sieges. In considering the composition of the engineer train, we must distinguish between siege *luxuries* and siege *necessities*.[1] To the former class belong trench railways and engines, steam apparatus for electric lights, and, in some cases, iron-band gabions. Thus, when we can get brushwood, it is evidently unwise to carry a ton[2] of gabion-bands for each gun of a train of 200 or 300. Nor can we always reckon on bringing up the machinery to be worked by steam sappers, even though the latter can transport themselves. Among the necessities, however, we must consider—in addition to the cutting and intrenching tools—the materials for the field telegraph, and, in certain cases, the means for the de-

---

[1] The lists should show these separately; and in all cases weights, volumes, and tonnage should be stated.

[2] 1,000 bands per gun is the number laid down; these weigh a ton.

molition and repair of railways; for the supply of water, and for the driving and ventilation of mines; as well as the explosives and apparatus for firing mines.[1] Again, supplies of timber for platforms, &c., may be necessities in some cases, while not in others, and so with the proportion of cutting tools. In the case of intrenching tools, the proportions must be based, not only on the largest number likely to be required, but also on their relative durability under the circumstances: for instance, shovels break down much sooner than pickaxes.

DUTIES OF TROOPS AT SIEGES.

In our service there is an urgent want of distinct and authoritative regulations on the duties of troops at sieges, such as exist in other armies. The duties of the troops are, either to work themselves, or to cover the workers. The sappers at a siege are, of course, too few to do the work, which must therefore be carried out chiefly by infantry. The main infantry working parties are demanded at head-quarters early each day, for the next day, by the Commanding Royal Engineer; and ordered in the orders for the day, in which also appears the detail of the covering parties, under the orders of a general for the day. In cases of emergency, it is necessary that small working parties should be obtainable from this general, on the demand of the Engineer Staff in the trenches.

As to what can be done, it is generally agreed that men can be employed for one day as covering troops, and on the next at work, leaving the third for rest; and, further, it is found that a man can do all he is capable of doing in one relief, in about five hours.[2] In

Working parties.

---

[1] A secure means of lighting Bickford's fuse is much required; also a good supply of tracing and other lanterns for work at night, as work will now, more often, be carried on under circumstances that permit the use of lanterns: our siege equipment only provides about 100.

[2] In the "Military Opinions of Sir J. Burgoyne" we find short reliefs of six hours strongly advocated; and, to quote an older opinion,

Short reliefs.

this time, untrained men at two paces apart—the most convenient interval—can excavate 80 to 100 cubic feet. Hence when reliefs can be changed without risk, short periods seem best; the men being all tasked and marched off when done. Above all things the system of detachments is to be avoided. As a rule, the working parties, under their own officers, parade by companies or battalions; without belts, with rifles slung, bayonets fixed, a few cartridges in their pockets, and with filled water-bottles; without the latter, thirst may stop the work. They assemble at the intermediate depôts, where they get tools and instructions, and are conducted to, and started at, the work by the engineers. Previous to work, whenever time permits, men should have some practice at extending along a traced line, or on a traced battery, at the park; or at their cantonments if it save them fatigue.

The earliest siege works will be protected by the outpost line of the investment; but as the works protrude beyond this line, special troops are required to cover and protect them.

Covering troops.

The formation of the covering parties is, in general, a chain of double sentries, with supports, and main body or reserve in front of the work that is being done. As a rule the double sentries should have, between them, a light pick and shovel, of which each battalion has 150 sets. Thus one man can always be getting cover, while the other keeps a look out. The covering parties are, of course, chiefly infantry; cavalry, with field guns, may be in reserve, under cover, on the flanks.

Strength of besieging force.

The strength of the force required to supply the working and covering troops, is generally reckoned with a view to its furnishing three reliefs, each equal to the probable field force of the garrison.[1] But from

---

Marshal Saxe says, "The soldier who only works three hours a day does his business cheerfully, and is able to stick close to it." In the long winter nights before Paris in 1870, the Germans sometimes employed as many as four reliefs.

[1] Estimated by Brunner at two-thirds the garrison. Brunner suggests that the force to supply the covering troops should be two and a-quarter times, and that the army of investment be three times the strength of the garrison.

what we have already pointed out as to the effects on the attack, of the size of the fortress; it is plain that, in proportion as the fortress and its garrison are large, the strength of the covering reliefs may be relatively smaller. Bearing in mind that in 1854 we besieged Sebastopol with a force inferior to the garrison; and considering the retaining power of the new arms—as proved by the war of 1870-71—as well as the certainty of support from the investing troops on the flanks; it is thought that three reliefs, each of one-third to two-thirds the garrison, will in most cases suffice as siege troops; while a force of one and a-half to two and a-half times the garrison will be capable of conducting both siege and investment according to the greater or lesser size of the fortress; particularly if the garrison, as must usually be the case, be composed of inferior troops. The siege of Belfort[1] is a remarkable example of what can be done in this way. The investment, at first conducted on a circumference of twenty-five, and afterwards of eighteen miles, was effected by 8,000 infantry with the usual proportions of the other arms —a force only half that of the garrison—nor did the siege corps at any time exceed twice the strength of the latter.

When we come to consider the actual conduct of a siege now-a-days, we are at once met by a new feature which the besieger has to face. In discussing the subject of the investment, we saw that the progress of the assailant is barred, at a considerable distance from the fortress, by the power of the defensive artillery. This distance is generally too great for the effective beginning of the siege proper; so that the attack is obliged to use its siege guns at long ranges, to subdue the fire of the defenders' advanced posts and permanent works; and thereby to secure an advance on the place to within besieging distance, along the region selected for the operation. This was notably the case with the advanced villages and woods occupied by the French outside of Belfort in 1870-71, which had thus to be bombarded by the

First siege operations.

[1] Wolff, p. 415.

German siege guns, before they could be captured. Hence it is plainly of importance to occupy commanding positions for the line of investment enclosing this region, and for the first artillery positions. These will enable the investing troops, along the front of attack, to advance with the help of their field guns; and to win some more ground from the defenders than elsewhere; and so to throw forward their shooting line, as to cover the first artillery position.

<small>First artillery position.</small> The positions for first batteries will, according to Hohenlohe, be at from 2,000 to 3,300 yards from the heavy guns of the defence: distances, we may observe, which were in some cases nearly doubled before Paris in 1870-71. It must be clearly understood that, from the first, "forward" should be the watchword of the attack; and the works, whether of the investment or of the siege, should always be advanced as far as they can be without *great* risk: at the same time we have to consider what is *probable*, rather than what may be *possible*; thus we find that Brunner puts the limits of the first artillery position at from 2,000 to 4,000 yards, and recommends a preponderance of three guns to two; assuming that the defence can mount a gun to every fifteen yards of front bearing on the attack. At Sebastopol in 1855, the preponderance, as given in Todleben's account, was the other way; in our first bombardment on the 9th of April, 1855, we opened fire with 444 guns; the Russians, according to him, with 466. Fortresses do not, however, often have a fleet and arsenal to arm from; nor, as in this case, a garrison of 70,000 men to oppose to an investing force of 60,000.

On the whole, even with improved shooting, the difficulties of observation will in general limit the distance of the first batteries to about two miles from the permanent defences. The great depth of this belt (about three-quarters of a mile, to a mile) gives a very wide choice in placing the batteries—these, as regards their sites, may be classified as:—

1. Those which are to be made behind permanent cover, over which they are to fire by observation only, with the help of scales.

2. Those which are made behind existing and removable cover, and unmasked when required.

3. Those which have to be made in the open, and can only be covered artificially.

Of the 500 batteries said to have been thrown up in the war of 1870-71, the majority were made out of sight and unmasked; a proportion were formed behind permanent cover; very few indeed were thrown up in the open.

The new power of firing accurately by observation with directing scales, not only makes night firing more effective, but also renders concealment more easy; and yet, though in the war of 1870-71 the attack reaped great benefit by first using the method of firing from unseen positions, we have indications that, for the future, it must share this advantage with the defence. Thus, at Paris, the Germans entirely failed to silence the French mortar battery behind the embankment (thirty feet high) at the Issy Station; while at Belfort the method was still further used by firing over the citadel, over traverses, and from interior spaces over a distant parapet: this fire the German guns quite failed to subdue. Further we learn that Brialmont now proposes a "batterie basse" in his large works, consisting of a straight retrenched parapet at the gorge, parallel to, and with a crest three feet below, the crest of the front. From this unseen position it is intended to direct a powerful, high angle fire over the front attacked (fig. 40, pl. xxi.) from guns unseen by the assailant. It is believed that the bare nature of the site of our operations in the Crimea, coupled with the former inaccuracy of curved fire, has for years inclined us to forget that natural cover is generally available; and the more so the further we are from the fortress; owing both to the wider choice, and to the difficulty of clearing within a great distance from it. Hence it will almost always be possible to choose sites screened by woods, walls, &c., the fronts of which can be quickly cleared, if necessary, for direct fire, or else to suit the required elevation. The following situations should also be sought, viz.:—

Indirect fire.

Choice of sites.

1st. Those which, from the trace of the defences, are not much exposed to cross fire, and which will be concealed by collateral objects from enfilade fire, and are easily supported.

2nd. Those where the background, as well as objects in front, are in favour of concealment.

3rd. Those near roads suitable for bringing up the guns, &c., or where the ground is passable for them.

4th. Those where the soil is not likely to give trouble by its wetness or hardness, and where undulations and slopes may be turned to account to diminish labour and aid drainage.

5th. Those with a command over the place.

Sheltered positions.

The positions of the German batteries south of Paris in 1870-71 illustrate the first; thus the first batteries 2, 3, and 4 (pl. viii.) lay so, that, owing to the trace of the forts, and the restrictions caused by embrasures, only a few French guns could be brought to bear upon them; while the French brought such a cross fire on Nos. 5 and 6 that they had to be disarmed; elsewhere many of the batteries, those for instance between Bagneux and Cachan, were so covered by woods, &c., on the flanks that they were but little exposed to enfilade fire, while those at Chatillon were so screened by trees, that lines of sight had to be cut through them, in order to fire.[1]

Again, the position of the Versaillist batteries at Montretout in 1871, made them hard to hit; as the ground rose a little behind them, while the tops of some trees in front, were just enough cut away for sighting the guns.

At Strassburg, also, many of the batteries were hardly visible behind the slight undulations that concealed them.

Approaches.

The approaches too play an important part: thus, some of the commanding positions round Bitche could not be used in 1870-71, for want of roads, and because of the difficulties of the country.

Again, the difficulties of construction are often

---

[1] Gœtze, p. 124.

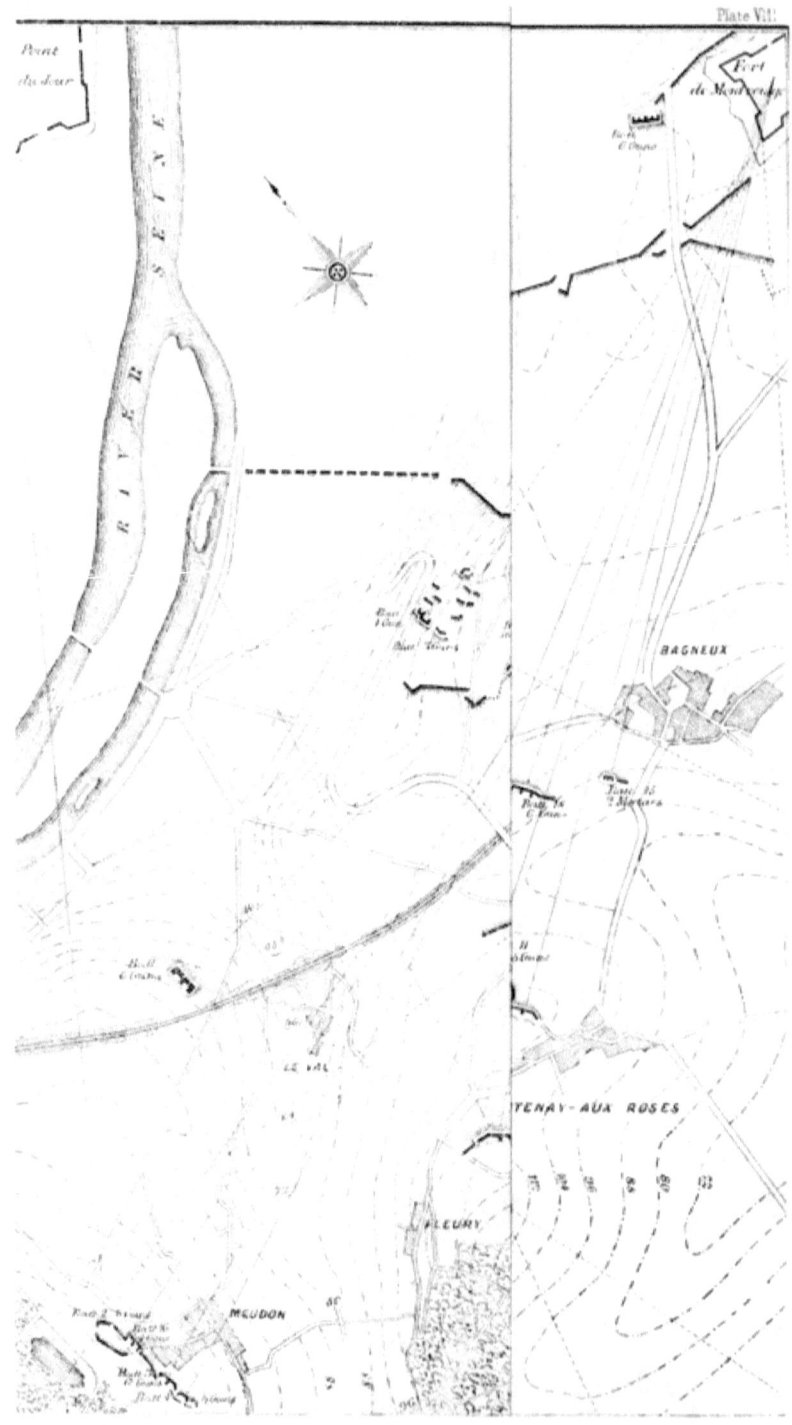

considerable. Those due to the rocky nature of the soil have already been referred to; and, in making the batteries before Delhi in 1857, fascines had to be used for want of earth. At the siege of Charleston in 1863, batteries in the marshes had to be floated on timber grillages; while in 1870-71, the sites chosen were mostly on high ground, and the wider area of choice, on the whole, diminished the difficulties.

Sites in woods or among buildings are also troublesome; but when the spot is important, these difficulties, and those of drainage, can be got over in the case of batteries made out of sight. Exposed sites should be so chosen, as to insure completion in a given time. In all cases the best engineering is to do the work with the least labour.

As to command, one great feature of the sieges in 1870-71 was that the increased range of the siege guns, had rendered available a number of commanding sites, till then too far off for the assailants' use.[1] This simplified the questions of defence and drainage.

Commanding sites for batteries.

The choice of sites is made jointly by the commanding officers of engineers and artillery: when chosen, the building of the unexposed batteries, and any necessary approaches to them, are begun as soon as the tools arrive, and without waiting for the siege guns. To be able to do this is a great gain: it saves the necessity of excessive working parties, and permits of much better work, and also prevents delays from unexpected difficulties. Thus, the blindages can be dug out to their full depth, and the timbers, rails, &c., properly placed; next, the terrepleins can be excavated, and the earth thrown on the blindages. The platforms are then laid and levelled without haste, after which the parapet is formed from the ditch, and the battery completed. From this it will be seen that, in general, two types of battery are wanted. The first, adapted for concealed sites, but which may afterwards be exposed to a heavy fire, should be arranged for execution in the number of reliefs that proves most economical of labour. In

Building of unexposed batteries.

Two kinds of battery necessary.

---

[1] Cf. Tables, P. P. R. E., vol. xx., pp. 22-26.

considerable. Those due to the rocky nature of the soil have already been referred to; and, in making the batteries before Delhi in 1857, fascines had to be used for want of earth. At the siege of Charleston in 1863, batteries in the marshes had to be floated on timber grillages; while in 1870-71, the sites chosen were mostly on high ground, and the wider area of choice, on the whole, diminished the difficulties.

Sites in woods or among buildings are also troublesome; but when the spot is important, these difficulties, and those of drainage, can be got over in the case of batteries made out of sight. Exposed sites should be so chosen, as to insure completion in a given time. In all cases the best engineering is to do the work with the least labour.

As to command, one great feature of the sieges in 1870-71 was that the increased range of the siege guns, had rendered available a number of commanding sites, till then too far off for the assailants' use.[1] This simplified the questions of defence and drainage. *Commanding sites for batteries.*

The choice of sites is made jointly by the commanding officers of engineers and artillery: when chosen, the building of the unexposed batteries, and any necessary approaches to them, are begun as soon as the tools arrive, and without waiting for the siege guns. To be able to do this is a great gain; it saves the necessity of excessive working parties, and permits of much better work, and also prevents delays from unexpected difficulties. Thus, the blindages can be dug out to their full depth, and the timbers, rails, &c., properly placed; next, the terrepleins can be excavated, and the earth thrown on the blindages. The platforms are then laid and levelled without haste, after which the parapet is formed from the ditch, and the battery completed. From this it will be seen that, in general, two types of battery are wanted. The first, adapted for concealed sites, but which may afterwards be exposed to a heavy fire, should be arranged for execution in the number of reliefs that proves most economical of labour. In *Building of unexposed batteries.* *Two kinds of battery necessary.*

---

[1] Cf. Tables, P. P. R. E., vol. xx., pp. 22-26.

such cases, parapets up to 30 feet thick may be provided, and such a thickness given to the earth roofs, as will render them secure. The second kind of battery, a number of which may have to be made on the same night, should be of such dimensions as can, with certainty, be thrown up in two short reliefs[1] (leaving room for future improvements); and can be executed with a *moderate* number of men. These batteries are intended for sites exposed to the defender's fire, particularly in the second artillery position; but they will also, if their earth roofs be thickened, answer quite well enough for most of the guns of the first artillery position.

Requirements of a battery.

The general requirements of a battery are:—

1st. A covering parapet and traverses; a screen, if exposed; a bomb-proof magazine having sheltered communication with the battery; bomb-proof, or at least splinter-proof cover for the detachments; ramps of descent for the guns; a space to store the loaded shells; a small observatory in the parapet for a "look-out," and a raised one for each group of batteries; and for those in, or just in rear of a parallel, covered communication behind them. It is, of course, understood as an invariable rule, that all the batteries of the position must open together. Hence, as the few batteries that must be made in the open, would be discovered in the daytime; their progress must, unless they are very distant indeed, be covered by an artificial screen, or else they must be begun and finished in one night. Artificial screens of branches, transplanted hedges, fascine walls, &c., answer the purpose in many cases.[2] Distant works were concealed, in the war of 1870-71, by laying green branches on

Artificial screens.

---

[1] The late Russian experiments showed that, if the range of a battery, not more than 1,150 yards distant, can be got by trial shots in the day, as many as 78 per cent. of the men working on it next night, might be hit by 20, 15 c. shrapnel shells.—*Revue d'Artillerie*, January, 1877, p. 346.

[2] Brialmont (vol. i., p. 201) mentions experiments in Belgium, which show that small green branches, not over $1\frac{1}{2}$ in. in diameter, do not fire percussion fuses; and, if the leaves are off, do not hinder the laying of guns. Time fuses could be fired through even thicker screens.

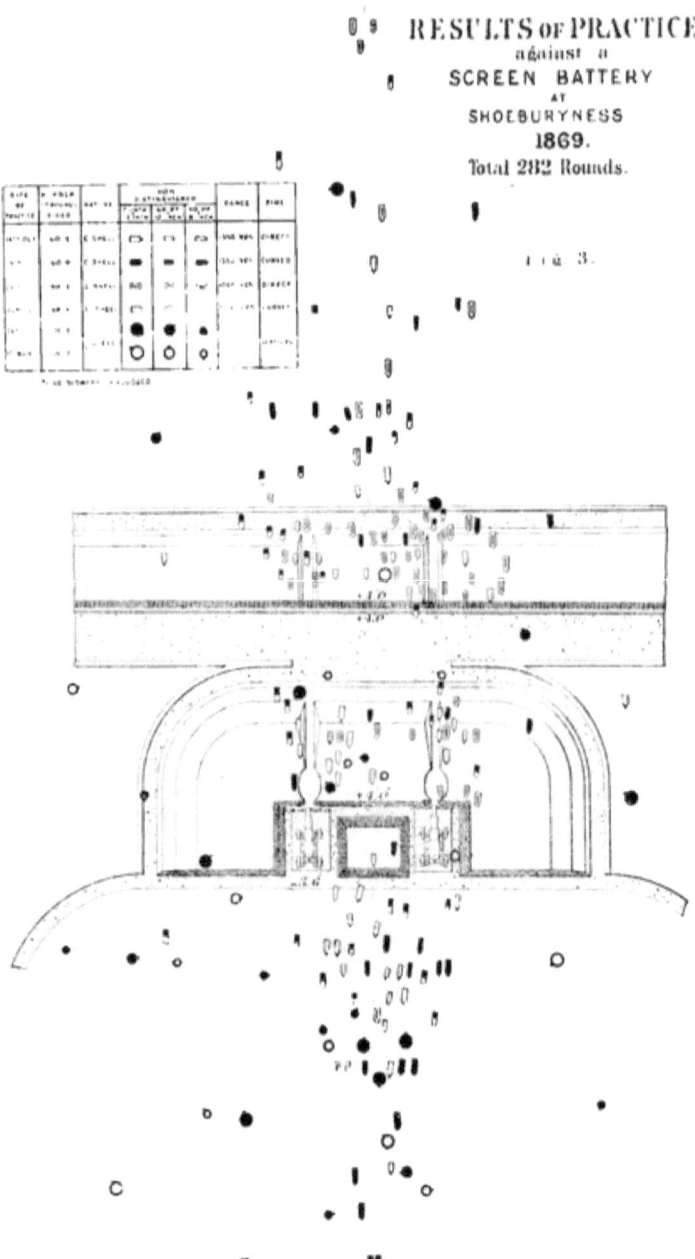

the fresh earth. This was done at the batteries between Bagneux and Cachan, south of Paris; at Soissons a similar use was made of snow. Again, we may use a continuous earth screen, like a parallel, long enough to make it doubtful where the battery or batteries are. This has, however, the disadvantage of disclosing the general lay of the artillery position, and, besides, adds considerably to the labour; while we can, by careful arrangement, throw up a good battery in one night, which we cover with a short screen; not so much to conceal the work in progress, as because experience shows that it is a most valuable protection, owing to the difficulty there is in distinguishing between it and the parapet (pl. ix.).

In 1870-71 the necessity of using screens was not forced on the Germans, though we learn[1] that batteries 6, 7, and 9, south of Paris, were provided with them. For direct fire, the screen is just high enough to let the gun be sighted over its crest, while for high angle fire, it may completely conceal the object from the battery. The usual section is a parapet with ditch and trench, revetted on the side of the battery, and distant 20 to 300 yards from its crest, as may best suit the ground and aid concealment; the greater distances being generally the more effective; and herein lies, as we think, an advantage the attack is likely to retain; for though the principle be adopted by the defence of concealing batteries within the works; the small depth of the works causes the positions of such batteries to be known within a little. In this respect the attack is much less limited, so that the defence will have relatively much greater difficulty in judging of the positions of unseen batteries.

One disadvantage of curved fire regulated by scales and observation is, that it is too slow for use against troops moving in the open; in which case, guns must be fired by sight. In considering this function of the siege artillery, we have to remember, that the capacity for a wide sweep of ground is chiefly im-

---

[1] Goetze, p. 174.

portant in the batteries of the first position; because, at the stage when those of the second position are formed, sorties will be met most successfully by the musketry fire of the parallels, and the artillery fire of the first batteries supported by field and Gatling guns.

On the other hand, the chief value of the screen is felt in the exposed batteries of the second position, where it will constantly be a necessity; while in those of the first, it may be dispensed with where it might impede the general action of the guns; this inconvenience in its use might be further diminished were the *fore-sight* on siege guns made so as to be raised and lowered, as well as the back-sight. For example, in the 64-pounder gun, the line of sight is 14 inches above the axis at the trunnions; accordingly, the gun can be sighted over a screen which just conceals it from the object; while the screen can always be placed so far forward, as to be cleared by a shell fired with any elevation. Thus, a shell fired with an elevation of 2 degs., would pass a foot above a screen placed 60 feet forward, and the crest of which was a foot above the

Raised sights. axis (fig. 23, pl. xx.). If, now, the sights could be each raised a foot, we could either employ a screen one foot higher, thus getting more cover; or, with the first screen, lay the gun on ground which, with the lower sight, would have been concealed by it. In fact, so great is the power of concealment which this method permits, even with direct fire, that, except where much depression is required, the whole of the assailants' guns, and indeed those of the defence, might be laid by sight, and yet be *unseen from the front*. This advantage will be much felt in preparing for the special battering guns already referred to, both on account of their having to fire direct, and because of the labour of making their emplacements, &c. In such cases, earth screens will act as blinds while the work goes on, and will afterwards conceal the guns themselves.

One-night battery. The general arrangement of a one-night battery is indicated in pl. x. The first step towards getting

Plate X

N.B. If 75 workmen per gun be not available for the one night batteries the parapets may be reduced to 20 ft from 27 ft & the intervals from 52 to 36 feet.

Fig. 2.

TABLE OF MEN REQUIRED.

1ST RELIEF.

R.E. N.C.O.s	Tasks	Diggers	Shovellers	Total
2	Front Ditch	40	36	76
1	Right Gun Portion and Ramp	18	6	24
1	Left do. do.	18	6	24
1	Shelters	14		14
1	Rear Trench	24	12	36
6	Total	114	60	174

2ND RELIEF.

2	Front Ditch	45	30	75
1	Gun Portion	12		12
	Shelters	8 Miners		8
	Rear Trench	24	12	36
3	Total	89	42	131

TASKS

1ST RELIEF.

Diggers	Length	Breadth	Depth	Contents C. Ft
A	4. 6	5. 0	4. 6	101.25
B	6. 2	3. 0	4. 6	83. 3
C	9. 0	4. 0	2. 9	99. 0
D	12. 0	8. 0	1. 0	96. 0
All others	5. 0	6. 0	3. 6	105

2ND RELIEF.

Diggers	Length	Breadth	Depth	Content C. Ft
X	6. 0	1. 6	3. 6	31. 6
All others	5. 0	6. 0	3. 6	105. 0

Working party averages 75 men per gun for each of 2 reliefs.

SECTION ON E.F.

a strong battery made in one night, is the arrangement of the diggers in the terrepleins back to back. This is further improved on, by excavating the terrepleins to a width of 12 feet only in the first relief, after which, the laying of the platforms is done at the same time as the terrepleins are being widened.

In fig. 2 the terrepleins are 3 ft. 6 in. below the surface, which would answer for high angle fire, or fire at a definite object; but for direct fire, when a wide sweep is required, if the platforms be at this depth, and the guns fire over 5 ft. 6 in., the parapets before the gun portions must be kept as low as 2 ft., gradually rising to 3 ft. between the traverses. The terrepleins would then be deepened to 4 ft., or more, around the platforms, the sides of the deepened portions being carefully revetted (figs. 25 and 30, pl. xx.). In addition, the guns would be concealed by a screen, arranged on the principle already explained.

This depth of 3 ft. 6 in. has been adopted, as it is a convenient limit for a single task. Platforms may now and then have to be laid on, or possibly above the surface of the ground for direct fire; but such cases are now more rare, and cannot be dealt with in one night. On the other hand, when the ground permits (fig. 22), the platforms may be at 5 ft. 6 in. below the surface, and in special cases even deeper (fig. 20), when channels to fire through, would be cut in the solid ground. Such arrangements permit the making of excellent blindages, which might sometimes even be mined out.

As at the present moment our siege guns, and those on naval slides, only fire over 3 ft. 9 in., and 4 ft. 3 in. respectively; we would, rather than use revetted embrasures, put them into batteries identical with those described for high carriages, but with the relative level of the crest and platform diminished by 2 ft., and we would depend on the concealment afforded by the screen, to protect the carriages.

The difficulty in making the battery (pl. x.) in two reliefs of four or five hours, chiefly consists in the trouble it takes to get the blindages excavated in time. In the majority of cases, where the work

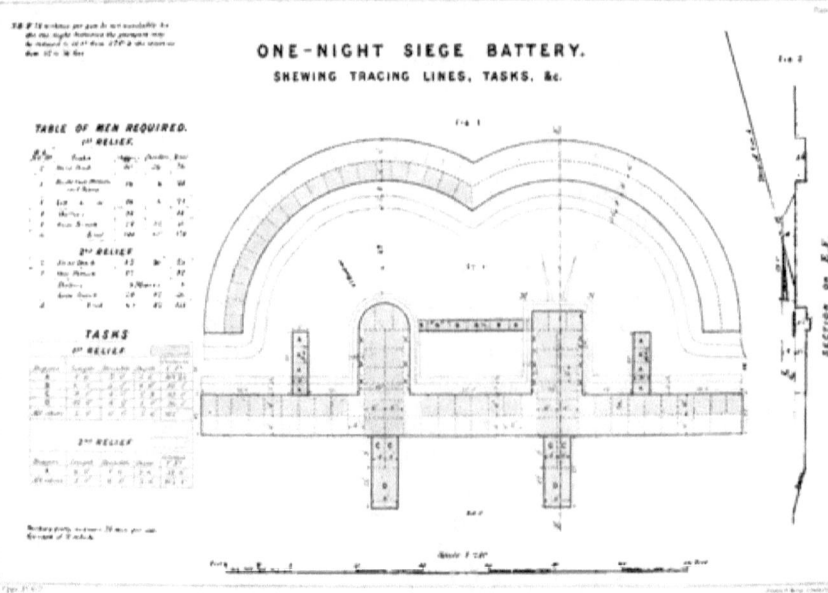

a strong battery made in one night, is the arrangement of the diggers in the terrepleins back to back. This is further improved on, by excavating the terrepleins to a width of 12 feet only in the first relief, after which, the laying of the platforms is done at the same time as the terrepleins are being widened.

In fig. 2 the terrepleins are 3 ft. 6 in. below the surface, which would answer for high angle fire, or fire at a definite object; but for direct fire, when a wide sweep is required, if the platforms be at this depth, and the guns fire over 5 ft. 6 in., the parapets before the gun portions must be kept as low as 2 ft., gradually rising to 3 ft. between the traverses. The terrepleins would then be deepened to 4 ft., or more, around the platforms, the sides of the deepened portions being carefully revetted (figs. 25 and 30, pl. xx.). In addition, the guns would be concealed by a screen, arranged on the principle already explained.

This depth of 3 ft. 6 in. has been adopted, as it is a convenient limit for a single task. Platforms may now and then have to be laid on, or possibly above the surface of the ground for direct fire; but such cases are now more rare, and cannot be dealt with in one night. On the other hand, when the ground permits (fig. 22), the platforms may be at 5 ft. 6 in. below the surface, and in special cases even deeper (fig. 20), when channels to fire through, would be cut in the solid ground. Such arrangements permit the making of excellent blindages, which might sometimes even be mined out.

As at the present moment our siege guns, and those on naval slides, only fire over 3 ft. 9 in., and 4 ft. 3 in. respectively; we would, rather than use revetted embrasures, put them into batteries identical with those described for high carriages, but with the relative level of the crest and platform diminished by 2 ft., and we would depend on the concealment afforded by the screen, to protect the carriages.

The difficulty in making the battery (pl. x.) in two reliefs of four or five hours, chiefly consists in the trouble it takes to get the blindages excavated in time. In the majority of cases, where the work is done at leisure, the excavations A and B should be dug out first, the latter being made at most 5 ft. wide, and all of them 6 ft. deep; and corresponding blinded recesses should be added on the outer sides of the terrepleins; but in the one-night batteries, the blindages cannot be made larger at the time, and can only be improved by laying timbers, &c., over the proposed enlargement, and afterwards mining it out and propping up the roof. In making these blindages, as indeed in all work of the kind, the load of the roof must be carried on uprights with their feet on the floor (fig. 41, pl. xxi.). No reliance can be placed on the support of the earth walls alone, even with long timbers.

Splinter-proofs and Bomb-proofs.

The conclusion come to after the Crimea, that an earth roof should be nine feet thick for perfect safety, though probably correct, has long been a heavy burden upon us; and the sooner we give up the idea of perfect safety in war the better; for in war, time and life being interchangeable quantities, the less valuable for the moment has to give way to the other; and the most we can hope for is to diminish, as much as possible, the percentage of loss. It is true that the 13-in. S. B. mortar had about the same penetration that the rifled 8-in. howitzer, or the 21-c. mortar has now, at ranges up to 1,500 or 1,800 yards, namely, 4 ft. to 4 ft. 6 in.; and at these ranges, with 5 feet of earth overhead, even timber roofs will often remain intact.[1]

Penetrations of shells.

We must not, however, jump to the conclusion that this is all we have to deal with. We find, as might be expected, that at very long ranges, the penetrations are much greater. Thus, among the effects observed in Paris in 1870, we learn[2] that, at Fort Issy, a 21-c. shell went through 6 ft. 6 in. of earth and 2 feet of arch ring below it; at the Double

---

[1] Thus 8-in. R. H. shells recently fired, at about this range, against blindages 4 feet wide, with good timber and rail roofs, covered with 4 feet of earth, in some cases penetrated to the roofs and blew them in: the earth, however, was favourable to penetration. With blindages of less width, the shells failed to penetrate.

[2] "Revue d'Artillerie," vol. iii., pp. 125-207.

Couronne shells pierced rail-blindages with as much as 6 ft. 6 in. of earth on their roofs; and at Forts Nogent and Vauves light timber roofs, with 6 ft. 6 in. to 8 ft. of earth above them, were pierced by 15-c. and 21-c. shells; the general conclusion come to being, that roofs of a single layer of logs are liable to be pierced, unless covered with almost 11 feet of earth; and that, even with short bearings and a double layer of 12 to 16-in. logs, 6·5 feet of earth overhead, is necessary against fire at such long ranges. These conditions are out of the question in one-night batteries, which are, however, seldom required so far from the fortress. In such batteries we cannot hope for more than 4 feet of earth on the blindages, and perhaps 5 feet over the magazines. In roofing magazines, &c., in the distant batteries, the above results should be remembered when they are exposed; but we may mention that the blindages and magazines of the German batteries had seldom more, and often less, than a metre of earth overhead,[1] and that in the whole war, in which 500 batteries were made, not a dozen magazines—if so many—were blown up by the penetration of shells.

In all cases when thin earth roofs are unavoidable, the span should be as narrow as possible; and such roofs may be further protected by rails or timber laid on the top of the earth, to explode the fuses and diminish the effect of the shells. The protection this affords, is pointed out in Thiers' account of the siege of Belfort, in which he mentions that he saved a badly covered blindage, by laying 8-in. logs on the earth roof. In the same way, paving stones were used on top of the earth roofs of magazines in Paris in 1870-71.

Against shrapnel and splinters even a foot of earth gives almost complete protection, an important fact, as it cannot be doubted that the improvements in shrapnel shell will make it very formidable to gun detachments.

The more advanced batteries, therefore, may be

---

[1] P. P. R. E., vol. xx., paper v., pl. ii., figs. 22, 23.

the better for light blindages in addition, in rear of the traverses and epaulements; and when the earth is rocky or frozen, parados in rear of the battery are also wanted as a protection from the splinters that come back.[1] In such cases, too, a supply of loose earth in rear of the trench, is convenient for filling the sand-bags required to make good any breaches in the parapets, or to fill shell-craters over the blindages.

Magazines. On the subject of magazines, there are also several points to be noticed:—

1st. As to their position. Since the Crimea we have considered the space in rear of a traverse as the best place, partly, no doubt, because with smooth-bores firing directly and at short ranges, the body of the parapet gave no little protection. Now-a-days however untrue the range may be, there is seldom much error in direction.[2] Thus the rectangle of the 21-c. mortar is said to be about 83 by 17 yards at a range of 3,000 yards, and that of the short 15-c. gun,

Their position at 4,360 yards, is reckoned to be about 93 by 17 yards: at such ranges the drop of the projectiles is so great, that anything that would hit a magazine in rear, is not stopped by the parapet of the battery. Hence we should like to see the magazine always put to one side of the battery, and connected with it by a narrow trench, if possible, 5 feet deep. If, however, there be many guns in one battery, some of the magazines must be in the traverses. The Germans, in 1870-71, always put their magazines to one flank.[3] The French, in some of the batteries in the Bois de Boulogne, in the second siege of Paris, still placed them behind.

As we have already mentioned, it will not, it is thought, be necessary to provide space for more than 100 to 160 cartridges for each gun; and as these will be in metal-lined cases, requiring only a width of 4 feet, the difficulties of drainage are decreased, and a narrow chamber is admissible. The loaded

---

[1] Sand bag revetments, if frozen, are dangerous when struck; the bags, if connected by wire, keep together better.
[2] Brialmont, pp. 157, 182.
[3] P. P. R. E., vol. xx., paper v., pl. iii.

shells for the battery will be stored in rear of the epaulements, as it is found that, even if one be exploded by being struck, it does not explode others. A case or barrel, let into the revetment of the gun portion, is convenient for small stores, and a shelf there, for a few shells, is convenient. In all these cases, when railway bars can be spared from the broken railways, they will be found very valuable as roofing materials.

In considering the question both of parapets and platforms, we are apt to look upon a battery, as a place from which guns are to shoot in a single direction only, and to forget that many of the guns, at least in the first position, will have a variety of duties. This is more than ever the case, now that the siege guns of the first position are the mainstay of the attack, both in the offensive and defensive actions in which it engages; hence these guns should not only fire "overbank," but should also be capable of wide training. Owing to their having neglected this, the Germans, during the battle of Belfort, had to use gun teams to pull the guns out of the batteries on to the surface of the ground, whence they fired over the parapets, on a sortie.

For purely siege purposes, a training of 5 degs. on each side of the central line of fire is generally enough; and a Clarke's platform, capable of being traversed to this extent by means of side tackles, may prove convenient if it will only last; as it aids the running up of the gun when loaded. Where a wide area must be commanded, and where the guns are to be laid by scales referred to fixed marks on the platforms, it seems desirable that the latter should be *horizontal*. In such case, the recoil is to be checked by wheel and axle breaks, and in addition, by light handy wedges, placed some distance behind the wheels. With low charges and high angles of elevation, these means are sufficient; and in a 15-ft. gun portion, the platforms (figs. 27 to 29) permit of a total training of 47 and 73 degs., with a recoil not exceeding 9 feet. In the first, the loss of training is balanced by the advantage of having more space

Platforms.

deepened in front of the platform, which is also strongest under the gun-wheels. No satisfactory method of meeting the increased recoil of our heavy M. L. R. guns, with battering charges, has, as yet, been tried; but the use of a hydraulic buffer, attached to the carriage as high up under the gun as may be, and anchored to the parapet (figs. 23 and 25), promises to check the recoil in 5 or 6 feet: its action may be helped by the use of wheel-wedges with so slight a slope as to let the gun stand on them till loaded, as it does on a Clarke's platform, while the wedges give much greater freedom than the latter. In cases where the training required is slight, it may be simplest to lay the platform at a slope of 1 in 24. After recoil, the gun may be loaded by depressing the muzzle, and using a rope or jointed rammer; the running up being further aided by using tackles worked under cover. In the Austrian experiments at Steinfeld,[1] in 1874, the buffer was used at so great a disadvantage, and the anchoring was so bad, that failure was inevitable; though the buffer proved, in itself, a success. Unfortunately, the cases in which we shall require this aid are exactly those in which the difficulties of construction are greatest, namely, in some of the batteries of the second position; still, we take it, the fixing of anchors will be less troublesome than was the making of embrasures.

To the objection that rock or marshes would render the use of these means difficult, not much importance is attached. In the nature of things we are already denied such sites for one-night batteries; while, with leisure, the ordinary anchorages used in military bridging will suffice.

In the special cases in which 7-in. and heavier guns are used, they will, it is thought, be mounted on level platforms, on naval slides if from the navy, the trucks running on bed-plates, or else on slides, on chocks, pivoted on an actual front pivot, and worked by side tackles. Heavy rifled howitzers (from 8-in. upwards) will, probably, be fired off beds

---

[1] "Revue d'Artillerie," vol. iii., p. 119, and vol. iv., pp. 60-65.

with directing bars or modified slides, and on level platforms. To secure the front pivot, it should, in all cases, be anchored somewhat as in fig. 22. Hydro-pneumatic carriages require an anchorage secured to the axle (fig. 17); a heavy baulk under the wheels, and a few planks under the trail.[1]

It must be admitted, that a breech-loader compares more favourably with a muzzle-loader, when used in a siege battery than anywhere else. The fact that with less recoil, that recoil is at once used by the employment of wedges to return the gun to the firing and loading position, is alone a great gain; while with a muzzle-loader, the muzzle of the gun must be several feet from the parapet in order to load, after which, the men have the labour of depressing and elevating, and of running up each time. However, our guns are muzzle-loaders with many points in their favour, and our business is to fit batteries to them. *Advantages of Breech-loaders.*

For the more distant batteries, or with high-angle fire from unexposed batteries, it may be better to lay the platforms so far from the parapet that the guns can be loaded in the firing position. In such cases the recoil could be utilized, as with a breech-loader, to run the gun up to its firing position.

In the sieges of 1854, 1863, and 1870-71, when great elevation was required for long ranges, special arrangements for lowering the trails were adopted, but they are, at best, clumsy expedients for doing what the carriage should itself permit. The new German siege carriages have been made to allow of elevation up to 40 degs. *Special platforms. Carriages for high-angle fire.*

In batteries made at leisure, gabions do well for the traverses, and strong hurdle revetments[2] extending from the terreplein to the crest are used for the fronts of the gun portions. *Revetments, &c.*

All these revetments require to be securely anchored, or they are of little use. Our siege train provides 2 tons of No. 14 wire for each army corps. A good deal of it, as well as spare fence or telegraph

---

[1] For diagrams of this carriage, see "Revue d'Artillerie," March, 1876, pl. xi.

[2] P. P. R. E., vol. xx., paper vi., fig. 1, pl. 1.

wire, should be used for this purpose with log or fascine anchors.

Look-out posts.

The "look-out" post for the man who signals "shell," is a niche at M or N revetted with a curved hurdle, and with steps to get up to it. In the Engineer Account of the siege of Sebastopol, the want of these steps is mentioned as a great inconvenience.

In those batteries which are to remain unseen, it is to be remembered, that the hostile shells are not likely to approach with a less drop than the elevation of the pieces in the battery. Thus, supposing the elevation required to clear an undulation in the ground to be 14 degs., the hostile shells would have a drop of at least 1 in 4 (fig. 2, pl. x.), and nothing would be gained by making the parapet thicker than about 19 feet. This principle applies in a degree to all batteries; hence the more direct the fire, the greater should be the thickness of the parapet, within reasonable limits, say up to 25 or 30 feet.

Other accessories now rendered necessary by the wide intervals that may separate the batteries and the parallels, are storm-proof posts, with abundance of splinter-proof accommodation[1] for the infantry detachments told off to protect the batteries.

Night of arming.

As batteries are completed, the guns are gradually got into those that are masked. Very heavy guns may have to be brought up on tramways; otherwise they come up over the open, or on made tracks, along pre-arranged lines, so as not to cross. Those for the one-night batteries are got in as soon as the platforms are down the next morning. The movement of guns cannot, according to Hohenlohe, be heard by the defence at a greater distance than 1,000 or 1,500 paces.[2]

During the night, before opening fire, the engineers clear away any natural screens which have to be removed; such, for instance, as the trees which

---

[1] Todleben mentions that, in Sebastopol, each man required about five square feet of floor space in such blindages. See also Goetze, vol. i., p. 119.

[2] Under the most favourable circumstances, identical sounds are heard four or five times as far off, as under the least favourable.

screened the German batteries on the plateau of Chatillon, south of Paris; and the poplars before their batteries at La Fère, in 1870-71.[1]

At dawn, and by a pre-arranged signal, all the guns open together, at a fixed rate of firing. *Opening fire.*

This bombardment of the advanced posts and the works of the defender, will be continued until the defensive fire is so far overpowered, that the covering troops can drive in the defenders, either step by step, or by a general engagement, as may seem best. Under cover of the first artillery position, the advance is made to about the extreme limit of the effective musketry fire of the defender, say 800 to 1,000 yards from the place; where the covering troops establish themselves in shelter trenches, &c.

At this stage, the state of things can be better seen, and the details of a further advance decided upon.

In the attack of a chain of forts, it will be necessary to make a gap large enough to secure the safety of a further advance on the interior defences. Thus Brunner suggests that it will be necessary to capture three forts, and silence the two that flank them; in attacking Paris in 1870-71, it was decided to advance against Issy and Vanves, and to silence Montrouge: in this case the elbow of the Seine would have given some protection to the left of an advanced attack. At all events two or more forts must be attacked: against each, a system of approaches will now be directed, strengthened at intervals by parallels. The first of these, under the protection of a superior artillery fire, can now be thrown up, either a little within, or somewhat beyond the limits of the defensive musketry fire; say between 700 and 1,500 yards from the works: the superior limit in the days of smooth bores having been about 600 or 700 yards. It is plainly desirable to open within the limits of musketry fire; because the distance is sure to be too great to allow the defender to hinder the first opening by *Extent of attack.* *First parallel.*

---

[1] Gœtze, vol. i., p. 208.

musketry fire, at night, from the defences: while the diminution in range, adds little to the efficiency of his shrapnel and Gatling gun fire. On the other hand, it gives the attack the power of using the first parallel as a *musketry position* against the defences. The Prussian regulations, based, perhaps, on a too favourable experience, put the first parallel at 659 yards from the works. Hohenlohe, and the writer in the "Militair Wochenblatt," suggest 833 yards (1,000 paces), while Brunner makes the distance to be from 995 to 1,660 yards. The first parallel at Strassburg in 1870, was opened at about 660 yards from the fortress. That against the Perches, before Belfort, was about 720 yards from those works, which were only armed with field guns (pl. xviii.).

In spite of this increased distance, the increased range of small arms, and the efficiency of shrapnel,[1] make the task more difficult than at the shorter distance, which in former days was only within the range of cannon shot. For this reason, it is important that the night of the operation be, as far as possible, unknown to the defence; and the outposts should, for several nights beforehand, endeavour to drive in the defenders' sentries at other points, as well as along the front of attack. On the night the parallel is to be thrown up, the task of protecting the work is given to a body of covering troops, who are on duty for twenty-four hours. Until the works are in such a state as to be exposed to injury, patrols and sentries alone, who give warning of an enemy's approach, may be sufficient: but it is seldom wise to let a sortie reach the works. In general, the formation of the covering troops is similar to an ordinary defensive formation, modified to suit the special circumstances. In addition to patrols in front, it consists of three lines, 1st, 2nd, and 3rd, the first composed of a line of double sentries, as close together as need be to prevent any hostile patrol from passing, and about 300 paces before the proposed parallel; while 100 paces in

Covering troops.

Formations for covering troops.

[1] See "Giornale d'Artilleria e Genio," part ii., pamphlet 6, 1874, and "Revue d'Artillerie," December, 1874.

rear of the sentries come their supports; these, as the attack will be made at night, are kept in small groups instead of being in line. Their strength, as well as that of the 2nd line, or main supports 100 paces in rear of them, may be about 1 man to a pace. Lastly, there is a third line, or local reserve of all arms, numbering about a man to every two yards of front occupied by the covering troops: this is massed 500 to 1,000 paces in rear of the ends of the parallel; and makes a total of, perhaps, 4,000 men to a mile.

For facility of command, these covering troops are divided into different sections from front to rear, each under one chief; and when the working and covering parties can be taken from the same unit, the former work with more sense of security. The positions for the outposts are decided by the engineers with reference to the future works, so that any intrenchments done by the outposts may work into the general scheme. In all cases, a clear understanding should be come to, as to the rallying points for the covering and working parties, should a sortie succeed in advancing.[1]

<small>Rallying points.</small>

After the supports are posted the parallel is traced.

The covering troops for the second parallel are in the same formation; but, for want of space, the interval between the sentries and the parallel is less; the sentries being about 150 paces to the front of, and the second line about 50 paces behind the parallel. The cover made by the sentries, in this case, will be occupied next night as rifle-pits. The heads of the saps and of advanced approaches are generally covered by groups of riflemen in pits in front of them.

For these trench works the working parties parade at the intermediate depôts, where they get tools, and whence each party marches (left in front if the extension be to the right, and *vice versâ*) to the point

<small>Working columns.</small>

---

[1] The siege train provides a printing and a lithographing waggon with each army corps: free use should be made of these, in order to furnish officers taking parties into the trenches, with instructions and sketches of the works.

from which it is to extend; the formation being a column of half companies, if the column consist of two or more companies; or, if of one, a column of sections: the latter being the more handy formation. Each column should have its reserve working party of ten per cent., which follows it in rear, with ten per cent. of spare picks and twenty per cent. of spare shovels: this is posted a little in rear of the centre of its extended column.

Reserve.

The formation of working columns in single ranks, is a novelty apt to confuse the infantry, and they should therefore adhere to the usual two-deep formation. Previous to the arrival of the columns, the parallels and approaches will have been traced by officers, who place markers instead of pickets, as was formerly the custom, to indicate changes of direction, and also to mark the extension points; at half company, or sectional, distance in rear of each of the latter, another marker is placed to show the halting point for the column.[1] As each column reaches its marker (fig. 32, pl. xxi.) it is halted, and the half companies or sections are moved off in succession by fours from the right (or left). The column of fours at once wheels to the left (or right) till it nears the traced line, when it again wheels to the left (or right), and *forms* to the right (or left) along the line, in single rank and at two paces' interval; the men having been previously warned, that the files are to extend at four paces' interval. With small columns the sections may be moved up in files, instead of in fours. By this method, the continuity of the stream will, it is thought, be better secured than by the German plan (fig. 31, pl. xxi.) of wheeling a column of sections along the rear of the traced line, and feeding that line from men from the inner flank of the leading section. The extension of the columns along the approaches is made from rear to front, and in a similar way; care being taken to place the first files exactly right at each change of direction.

Extension of working columns.

The chief alterations that, for the present, seem

Alterations now required in siege trenches.

---

[1] Or 2 markers 10 paces apart for a double extension.

desirable in the first parallel and approaches, and more or less in all the trenches, are:—

1st. An increase of depth from three to four feet.

2nd. The provision, where steps are wanted, of built-up fascine steps.

3rd. The addition of deep shelter trenches, some fifty paces in rear of the parallel, for the guard of the trenches.

The necessity for increased cover has led to the first; at the same time, the increased length of trench work[1] makes it all the more necessary to utilize any shelter trenches thrown up by the covering troops, and to turn existing cover to account wherever it will answer instead of earth work. In addition, as advanced batteries will be rare, it will seldom be necessary to have the whole parallel fit for wheeled transport, so that large portions may be left unwidened: thus, in the Versaillist trenches in the Bois de Boulogne in 1871, parts only were widened after the first relief. Narrow parallels.

Again, earth steps constantly break down if much used, and are troublesome to cut; and further, the trench can be defended, before the building of the fascine steps, by getting up on to the reverse, and firing over the parapet; or in the case of the first relief by jumping, if necessary, from the reverse on to the berm.

The fact that any trench arranged for shooting now gives imperfect cover, has made it necessary to use additional trenches for *shelter only* for the guard of the trenches. These trenches are too deep for shooting, and may even be roofed and blinded.[2] Those at the siege of Soissons in 1870 were dug 100 paces behind the parallel, which was itself 900 yards from the place. Shelter trenches.

The guard of the trenches is the force that holds and defends them. It is composed, as usual, of a first line, supports, and reserves in proportions somewhat similar to those of the covering troops. Guard of the trenches.

[1] Even at Sebastopol the English trenches were, it is stated, twelve miles in length. (Engineer Account.)

[2] " R. E. Essay," 1875, pl. v., and P. P. R. E., vol. xx.

The first line, consisting of a man to every two or three paces, holds the parallel with one-third of its strength disposed as double sentries on the berm; the remainder being in shelter a little in rear, or else in the parallel. The main supports lie under cover, being 200 or 300 paces in rear at night, and further back in the day. The reserve is about 600 to 800 paces to the rear at night, and 2,000 to 2,500 paces in the day-time.

The assailant being thus established in the first parallel, the sorties of the besieged are driven to attacks on the flanks, which are favoured by the salient position of the siege works with reference to the general line of investment; and against such the flanks must be specially protected by defensive localities, or, in their absence, by small works prepared for infantry and mitrailleurs rather than for guns, which are more favourably placed further to the rear.[1]

Second artillery position.
After the parallel is completed and connected by approaches with the intermediate depôts, steps are taken to bring forward the guns into second artillery positions in the neighbourhood of the first parallel, whence they can deal systematically and in detail with the defences; that is, dismount guns, demolish cover, breach the escarps, and sometimes destroy the defences in the ditches. The sieges of the war of 1870-71 have shown that, with the best artillery then used, the two first objects can seldom be effected, with a reasonable expenditure of ammunition, at ranges exceeding 1,500 or 1,600 yards; while for breaching with curved fire, we shall endeavour to show that the corresponding limit appears to be about 1,400 yards. Nor in this case must the distance be less than 750 to 900 yards.

One of the most marked points of difference between the sieges of the past and present lies in the fact that, at these distances which are more or less beyond the range of the defenders' musketry, the work of the artillery can, with certain exceptions,

[1] The preparation of such localities is dealt with in detail, in the "R. E. Essay" of 1875.

be almost entirely completed. These exceptions are the cases in which use is made of very light guns to complete and maintain the suppression of the defenders' fire, and of light rifled or S. B. mortars, which are advanced as the works progress. This general fact is of great importance, both in simplifying the construction of the close approaches and decreasing, on the whole, the loss in the batteries.[1] The batteries of the second artillery position will, in general construction, be like some of those of the first. They will, however, be exposed to a more accurate, more powerful, and more sweeping direct fire, and to a more accurate, though less penetrating, high-angle fire. Hence the importance of even more overhead cover and of thicker parapets. At the same time the means of concealing their construction will be fewer. More of them may have to be made in the open, and when made, the guns will be exposed especially to the effects of light field guns, of wall pieces, and of musketry, unless when screened. If exposed to enfilade fire, it may, on the whole, be better to raise the traverses above the height of the parapet; though, with a view not to present a notched sky-line to the front, the elevation of the traverses should blend gradually with that of the parapet before the guns. Under these circumstances, it is thought that the exact positions of guns unavoidably exposed, and of the raised traverses, may be concealed by a narrow open net running along the whole crest of the battery, and hung on a telegraph wire supported on sticks in the parapet. This net would not prevent the process of laying, and could be raised to run up and fire.[2] Guns, concealed from direct fire, may be protected from shrapnel by the ordinary casemate rope mantlets, supported above the crest of the parapet.

Increased exposure of the second batteries.

Concealment of guns.

When the defences are ill traversed, and exposed to enfilade; when the parapets are weak and cut up

Direct fire desirable.

[1] "The Germans, in the siege of Paris, had only 339 men killed and wounded in their siege batteries."—BRIALMONT, vol. i., p. 255.

[2] Guns en barbette would attract less attention, if painted to match the parapet.

by embrasures; when the masonry is exposed, or when the works of the defence are only temporary in their nature; direct and enfilade fire with high charges, produce the greatest effects; because, the velocity on impact being great, and the drop small, great grazing and striking effects are produced.

When, therefore, direct fire is suitable, and can be used, it should always be resorted to. It appears, however, to be sometimes forgotten that guns, firing direct, are often exposed to be silenced by direct fire; and also that they must have an object to fire at. As long as the range is such that an elevation of 6 degs. or more is required, guns can be fairly concealed by shallow countersloping embrasures: but, at short ranges, they can only be laid, with ordinary sights, either through deep embrasures, or over-bank; two methods which Todleben, after the late extensive trials, declares to be "No longer admissible at present."[1] In this direction, it must be granted, the defence has relatively gained: for, as pointed out on page 19, it has at its disposal, methods of mounting that, at the same time, allow the guns to fire direct, and secure them from direct exposure. The attack, on the other hand, will, it seems, be more and more denied the use of direct fire; unless means be found either of providing it with disappearing carriages, or with raised sights; or unless it can so master the fire of the place, as to be able to expose its own guns without risk. Again, in good modern works, the trace provides against enfilade, and the disposition of the guns is such, that nothing but masses of earth are exposed to direct fire. The escarps, too, will not only be unseen, but will be secure against shells falling at considerable angles; and the ditches will depend for flank defence, on sunken caponiers, or *drop* galleries, with well-covered roofs.

Under these circumstances, the importance of curved or high-angle fire is constantly increasing with the increasing difficulties that the artillery have to overcome. What we are chiefly concerned with is *what*

[1] "Revue d'Artillerie," November, 1876, p. 140.

the guns can do, rather than *how* their work is done. We cannot, however, avoid a reference to the latter.

The terms *curved* and *high-angle* fire are of course only relative, but it seems customary to apply them to cases where charges lower than the service charges for direct fire, and elevations higher than those corresponding to these charges, are used; also to attach the idea of greater elevation to the latter, than to the former: *vertical fire* is a term applied to high-angle mortar fire. Curved fire.
High-angle fire.
Vertical fire.

Curved fire is used:—

(1) To clear a screen in front of, and generally near the battery, which is placed behind it for the sake of cover, as we have already noticed, or of necessity.

(2) To fire over an intervening object close to, and concealing the target.

Cases may occur when both difficulties are combined, but these so complicate the problem that they should be avoided.

In the second case curved fire is used for:—

(1) Enfilade, (2) demolitions, (3) breaching.

For all these purposes it may be assumed, that the greatest velocity on impact should be aimed at, which, as regards the shell, is obtained by its being long relatively to its diameter; and also (except when horizontal roofs have to be pierced) the smallest possible drop; because accuracy and penetration decrease with the velocity, and in proportion as the drop increases.

Antiquated works, badly traversed, may be enfiladed at sufficiently low angles; but with good modern traverses, close together, the drop, at short ranges, has to be too great to get good striking velocity. Hence the traverses have to be cut down somewhat with full service charges, or enfiladed from the first positions at long ranges and high angles, in which case the striking velocity will be sufficient, though the expenditure of ammunition may be large. Enfilade curved fire.

For (2) if the surface to be struck be horizontal, as in the case of magazines and casemates, and vertical penetration be required; a very high-angle fire, at the Demolition curved fire.

greatest range that allows of accuracy, should be used.[1] For these purposes, when transport permits, it would be well to have in the train a few 10-inch R. howitzers, on account of the greater power of their shells.

For vertical surfaces the conditions are the same as for (3), and as an example we may mention the demolition of the keep and gorge walls of Lunette 44 at Strassburg (figs. 10 and 13, pl. xi.).

When enough of the surface to be destroyed can be seen from a distance, direct fire with full charges should, of course, be used in preference to curved fire. Thus at Soissons, in 1870, the Germans breached a revetment, half of which was seen, at a range of 1,830 yards, and at an angle said to have been as oblique as 45 degs., by the direct fire of long 15-c. guns.

Breaching by curved fire.

Breaching by curved fire was first used, by accident, in enfilading a ravelin at Alessandria in 1799. We in England were the first to experiment on it by breaching a Carnot wall (fig. 6, pl. xi.) at Woolwich in 1824; but since then we have left the subject to our continental neighbours, whose trials[2] were put in practice in the wars of 1859 at Borgo-Forte, and of 1870-71, and whose siege trains are supplied with guns specially intended for the purpose, the shooting of which has been tabulated for practical use.

Method of horizontal and vertical cuts.

The method used till lately for breaching an escarp was to make a horizontal cut in the wall at one-third

---

[1] Experiments have shown that a casemate arch-ring, 1 metre thick, is proof against 21-c. R. M. shells fired at short ranges and high angles, if covered with three or four feet of earth. That an arch-ring of the same thickness, with six feet of earth above it, is proof against the 28-c. (11·2 in.) B. L. R. mortar, fired at short ranges; and that an 18-in. arch-ring of 14 ft. span, with 2 ft. 6 ins. of concrete above it, is proof against the 350 lbs. shell of the 10-in. R. howitzer at 3,000 yards range, and falling at 47 degs. The last fact makes it doubtful that the addition of a few feet of earth is an advantage.

[2] For instance, the Austrian experiments at Verona in 1862; those of the French at Aix in 1863. The Prussian experiments at Schweidnitz in 1857; at Jülich in 1860; at Stettin and Silberberg in 1869; and, since the war of 1870-71, those at Graudenz in 1873 (P.P.R.E., vol. xxii.). Pasley (p. 376) describes the experiment of 1824.

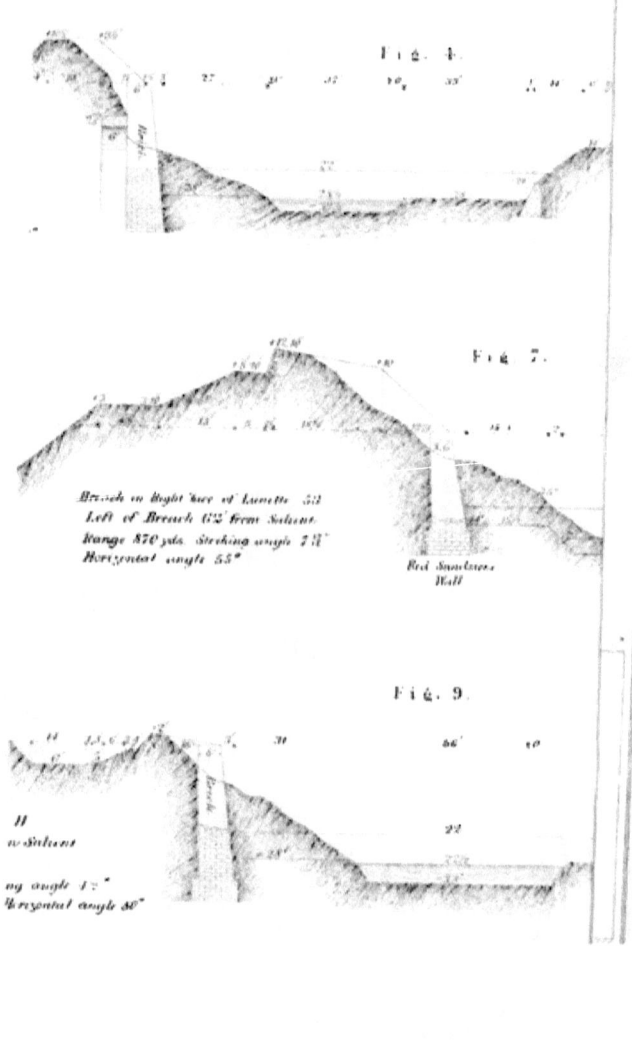

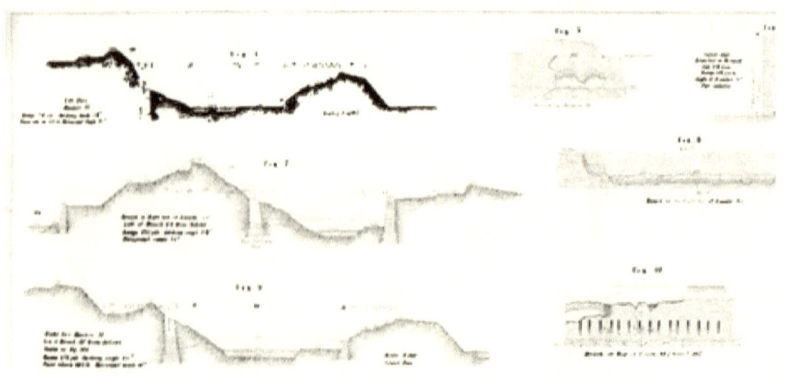

Pl. XII.

BREACH IN RIGHT FACE OF BASTION IV. MADE BY SHORT 15 C.M. GUNS.
Range 800 Yds.-Horizontal Angle of Fire 75° - Angle of Descent 4° - Striking Velocity 775 F
First 3 days firing, Rounds 500—Hits 274—(including 2 earths)
(*The Squares on the Target are Metres.*)

BREACH IN RIGHT FACE OF BASTION IV MADE BY SHORT 15 C.M. GUNS.
Range 800 Yds.- Horizontal Angle of Fire 75°- Angle of Descent 4°- Striking Velocity 775 Ft
Total Number of Rounds Fired 680 — Hits 624, (including 36 earths.)
(*The Squares on the Target are Metres.*)

of its height from the bottom,[1] and to bring it down
by a pair of vertical cuts at the ends, as was done in
breaching the right face of Bastion 11, and the left
face of Bastion 12 at Strassburg in 1870[2] (figs. 4 and
9); or by battering the face of the wall upwards from
the horizontal cut, as the French did at Aix; and as
happened unintentionally in the breaching of Lunette
53 at Strassburg, owing to the difficulty of regulating
the firing.

More recent experiments have (pls. xii. and xiii.)
shown that, at all events with the 15-c. B. L. gun,
the mean point of impact for the horizontal cut need
not be more than half the way down, and the lowest
point of impact a little more than half the way down,
in proportion as the angle of descent is small (fig. 34,
pl. xxi.). At the same time, the method of breaching
by demolition from the cordon downwards, has been
tried with complete success (pls. xiv. to xvi.). So much
so, that General Count Byland-Rheidt writing on
curved fire in 1874, remarks: "We are, therefore,
justified in the opinion, that the method of demolish-
ing the upper half of the scarp, by means of curved
fire, will, in future, supersede the old plan of can-
nelure cutting."

For breaching by means of horizontal and vertical
cuts, an accurate knowledge of the profile is required,
and also means of observing the effects, particularly at
the completion of the horizontal cut. In addition,
the proportion of hits must be large, and as this cannot be secured with high angles of descent and low
velocities, owing to the great vertical and lateral
spread, the method has been found impracticable in
cases where, in order to strike halfway down the
wall, the drop must be over 14 or 15 degs., and difficult with angles of over 8 or 9 degs. Hence, as in
new works the cordon of the escarp is placed at

---

[1] In early days, when the work of breaching was done from the
counterscarp, the rule was to cut through the wall, at such a height
from the foot, that men could mount, even were the débris removed.
This would seldom be possible now: at the same time the removal of
the débris is now more difficult under shrapnel fire at night.

[2] Decker.

a drop of from 12 to 15 degs. with reference to the covering mass, the drop to a point halfway down the wall, would be too great to allow of the cutting of a horizontal groove there.

Breaching by demolition.
On the other hand, the experiments at Graudenz, in 1873[1] (pls. xiv. to xvi.), showed that a breach can be formed by battering from the cordon downwards; provided that the lowest point of impact be taken one half, and the mean point one quarter, instead of half the way down, as in the case of the first method. Hence, though, in the latter case, the lowest shots must strike nearly as low as in the first, the average of shots have not to fulfil as difficult conditions (fig. 35): consequently the same *accuracy* is not required—an important point in using M. L. guns for this purpose; for, however well they may shoot, it remains to be shown that, in such delicate work their shells, even when centred by gas-checks, can equal in uniform accuracy those of the truly centred B. L. shells. This decrease in the difficulty permits of the successful use of higher angles and lower velocities, and, therefore, of dealing with more difficult profile conditions.[2] This conclusion has, of course, reference to cases (fig. 33) in which the parapet is not retired from the cordon. Where so retired, or when the exterior slope is very gentle, breaching is rendered more difficult.

Limits of oblique fire.
Theoretically, as long as the striking velocity is sufficient, the effective limit to the angle of descent, measured with a vertical section of the wall (fig. 33), is the same as that of the horizontal inclination of the line of fire, with the face of the wall. This angle is known to vary with the hardness of the material, and is commonly between 55 and 60 degs. In breaching the soft red sandstone wall of Lunette 53, where

[1] P. P. R. E., vol. xxii.

[2] Müller (p. 24) puts the number of hits to each metre of breadth in the three breaches (pls. xiii. xv. and xvi.) at 63, 51·7, and 21·2; though the conditions in the first case were the least difficult. From the result of our sieges in Spain, Sir W. Denison shows that, with direct fire at 500 yards, it took about 345 24-pounder S.B. shot to the same breadth. Cf. P. P. R. E., vol. iii., art. 8.

BREACH IN RIGHT FACE OF RAVELIN III. MADE BY SHORT 15 C.M. GUNS.
Range 1155 Yds.—Horizontal Angle of Fire 57° 42'—Angle of Descent 7°—Striking Velocity 673 Ft.
Second Day. Rounds 360—Hits 224, viz :-(46 earths, 1 cordon, 177 wall.)
(*The Squares on the Target are Metres.*)

BREACH IN RIGHT FACE OF RAVELIN III. MADE BY SHORT 15 C.M. GUNS.
Range 1155 Yds.-Horizontal Angle of Fire 57° 42'.-Angle of Descent 7° Striking Velocity 673 Ft
Third Day, Rounds 484—Hits 336,-viz—(124 earth, 1 cordon, 211 wall.)
(*The Squares on the Target are Metres.*)

BREACH IN RIGHT FACE OF RAVELIN IV. WITH 21 C.M. HOWITZERS.
Range 1177 Yds.,-Horizontal Angle of Fire 58° 30.'-Angle of Descent $6\frac{10}{11}°$-Striking Velocity 705 Ft. Second Day, Rounds 190—Hits 132, (viz 59 earths, 3 cordon, 70 wall.)
(*The Squares on the Target are Mètres.*)

the line of fire was at 55 degs. with the masonry, the firing was observed from a captured counterscarp gallery, and, at first, many shots were seen to glance. At Silberberg, in 1867, against gneiss masonry, an angle of 57½ degs. was found too small; though not against the good brick masonry at Graudenz, in 1873. With the ordinary breaching velocities, but with such angles of descent, the striking velocity would doubtless be far too small, and the chance of hitting the target (A C, fig. 33) would be slight.[1] The lowest striking velocity that has been found to affect masonry is probably the final velocity of 475 feet, referred to in the case of Lunette 44 at Strassburg. For cutting a horizontal groove, Byland-Rheidt gives the lowest limit for the 15-c. and 12-c. guns as 630 feet and 866 feet. With heavier shells a somewhat less striking velocity, and a greater angle of descent will be effective; they may therefore be used at shorter ranges.

Striking velocity.

As to the limits of range for breaching by curved fire without undue expenditure of ammunition, those used at Graudenz, namely, 800 and 1,177 yards, are, so far, almost the extremes for revetments; at less than the first limit, the velocity on striking is apt to be too low; while much beyond the second, the dispersion, with high angles, becomes too great.

Limits of range.

Of course, as the conditions become more easy the distances may be increased; thus, in 1870, the short 15-c. guns in the German battery No. 19 breached the masks of two arches in a curtain of Fort Issy at 1,800 yards, and with only 200 rounds; the necessary drop was not, however, very great. A well known authority[2] puts the dangerous limit for masonry at 2,700 to 3,300 yards; a distance largely exceeded by the Americans at Charleston, where a breach was made in Fort Sumpter by direct fire, at ranges of from 3,428 to 4,290 yards.[3]

[1] It has been observed that a shell from an 11·2-in. rifled mortar fired at 1,460 yards, with an elevation of over 45 degs., on striking a revetment, only dented it about eighteen inches.

[2] Brialmont, vol. i., p. 157.

[3] The guns were 100-pounders, 200-pounders, and 300-pounders, and of the shots fired, 33 per cent. were hits.—GILLMORE, p. 64.

To return to the comparison of the methods of breaching; that by demolition has the further advantage that the débris will not, it is found, interfere with cutting down the wall to the depth required; while with the horizontal cut the débris may get in the way, as happened at Strassburg in 1870, at Lunette 53 (fig. 7, pl. xi.).

Again, the masonry brought down by demolition, falls in small pieces, and gets covered by the earth of the parapet; while by the other method it comes down in large troublesome masses, leaving any counter-arches standing, and supporting the earth (pls. xiii. and xv.): in the demolition method these latter are pounded, as well as the wall. In all cases the earth is afterwards brought down by salvoes of shells fired with reduced charges, large powder bursters, and slow fuses. The process of breaching would be rendered more easy if means be found of having a fuse in the base of the shell. With such a fuse, the greater penetration of Palliser shells could be turned to account. A time fuse which would stand the shock of impact would be best: at present they are apt to go off on impact; and are almost sure to do so against masonry, if the velocity be high: in which case too, loaded plugged shells do the same.

Slow fuses.

Gun-cotton. Gun-cotton as a burster was used with some success at Verona, in 1862. Since then the possibility of using wet compressed gun-cotton has been found out, and has rendered the use of gun-cotton for the purpose much safer; while the employment of dry cotton with the water shell shows that the proportion of dry cotton required for detonation can be used without risk. Hence it is anticipated that its employment for breaching purposes is only a question of time.

Proportions of ammunition. At Graudenz, the proportions of ammunition used with the short 15-c. gun and 21-c. mortar to make nearly similar breaches (pls. xv. and xvi.) were as 7 to 8. The heavier shells have, however, certain advantages already pointed out. On service the proportion would always be larger; thus, at Strassburg, the number of rounds in the three cases we have mentioned were: 1,000 for Lunette 53; 500 for Bastion 11; and 465 for Bastion 12; and it is to be remembered that these breaches were in a very incomplete state, and would have required a good deal more hammering to have made them practicable.

In breaching detached walls, or caponiers, the lowest point of impact is fixed as low as possible, and the mean point taken halfway between it and the top. It is supposed, apparently with reason, that the blow of a shell has much more effect on a detached wall than on a revetment, owing to the vibration set up in the former. As early as 1862, a detached wall at Verona was breached at 1,400 yards; the drop required having, in some cases, been as much as 17 degs.; and we further learn[1] that the Baden guns at Kehl, in 1870, breached a part of the citadel of Strassburg at the same angle, and at a range of about 2,200 yards. The destruction of the gorge wall at Fort Vanves, in 1870, is another instance. *Breaching detached walls.*

The demolition by curved fire of unseen dams in the defences was, for the first time, attempted at Strassburg in 1870.[2] The positions of the two most important dams, one before Curtain 15 and the other before Lunette 63, were only known approximately; and the point of impact was transferred by calculation, from a visible point to the dams, the gates of which were much injured, and would probably have failed under continued firing. Three 15-c. guns were used for this purpose in Battery 33, at a range of 1,950 yards, inclined to the dams at 63 and 44 degs. respectively, and with a striking angle and velocity of 7 degs. and 918 feet (pl. xvii.). *Demolition of Batardeaux.*

In future we may expect that similar weak points will be strengthened by iron plating.

We see, therefore, that with old fortresses, or in cases where the greatest drop need not exceed 10 to 12 degs. for revetments, and 15 to 18 degs. for detached walls, breaches can, at present, be effected *Possibilities of breaching with curved fire.*

---

[1] Brialmont, vol. i., p. 154.
[2] See a paper by Capt. Clarke, R. A., in "R. A. I. Proceedings," vol. viii.

by curved fire with a greater or less expenditure of ammunition; though the difficulty with revetments is considerable when the striking angle exceeds 8 or 9 degs. When much greater angles of descent would be necessary, the difficulty may be overcome, either by cutting away the covering mass—which can be done by shell fire to a depth of 4 or 5 ft.—or, if this be not enough, by blowing in the counterscarp, and exposing the wall or caponier.

As to the future, bearing in mind the facilities given by the demolition method, and the probability of greatly increased effects from the use of guncotton and of improved fuses, it is to be expected that breaching will become generally practicable, unless the lower half of the wall is more than 4 ft. below a line of fire passing through the crest of the covering mass, with a drop of from 12 to 15 degs. for revetments, and 15 to 20 degs. for detached walls,[1] and making a horizontal angle with the wall, of not less than 45 to 60 degs. according to the nature of the material; provided always that the effects of the firing *can be observed*.

Under these circumstances, walls, the cordons of which are covered from a drop of 1 in 4, will still be safe against curved breaching fire, unless very low, until the levelling of the covering mass. Generally the widening of the ditch for the caponier is a favourable place for breaching, particularly as the débris may help to smother the caponier.

As a rule, at least two breaches should be made, each as wide as possible, say 30 to 60 ft.[2] The formation of a breach should be postponed to the last, in order to prevent the defenders from retrenching or barricading it—as happened at Soissons in 1870, where the French bravely worked on the breach under a

---

[1] In the new forts at Strassburg, a line of fire perpendicular to the detached walls would need a drop of 17 degs. to reach even the top of the wall. The Austrians, after the breaching of a detached wall at Borgo-Forte, decided to cover walls from a drop of 1 in 4.

[2] In firing down narrow ditches, a slight increase in width of breach may be got, by letting the guns in battery cross their fire, as was done at Strassburg in 1870.

night fire of shrapnel—or even to stop the defenders from doing intentionally, what the assailant did by accident at Strassburg in 1870, namely, raising the covering mass artificially across the line of fire, provided a night be allowed them; in which case, also, progress might be delayed by laying rails, logs, &c., on the earth above the breach, to burst shells fired with the object of bringing it down.

Supposing, however, that breaches have been made, an assault cannot be risked, without learning that they are practicable, or that they have not ceased to be so, by the removal of the débris from the foot of the wall: this, if any respite were given, might be effected by laying a rail tramway along the counterscarp, from the breach to a convenient distance. Nor would it be practicable, even with the certainty of finding a breach, to advance any distance over the open, as long as the works are defended: hence it is evident, that breaching at long ranges, by no means lessens the necessity for advancing the siege works to the counterscarp; as soon, therefore, as the defenders' fire permits, further approaches are carried forward, and parallels made. During the war of 1870-71, the difficulties of the close attack, under modern conditions, were only in part experienced; because the power of resistance, even to a distant artillery fire, was so small that, except at Paris, there was no reserve of force left, to oppose the close attack. In the future, however, we may expect, that the defence will mend matters in this way, and that the contest with the second artillery position will be a severe one, before the attack gains the mastery; particularly if the defence succeed in maintaining their rifle fire from the parapets.

Necessity for close attack.

Still, the great increase of the effective range of musketry enables the defenders of each parallel to command a wide extent of ground to their front; hence the necessity for having five parallels and several demi-parallels, as described by some writers, is not anticipated, and it is thought that a second and third parallel, or portions of them, each at a rather greater distance from the fortress than from the preceding one, with short lengths of lodgments from the approaches, will bring us close to the glacis; beyond this, if mining be necessary, a mine lodgment must be made, and an advance made by mining; while, in the absence of mines, the advance will be by sapping till the counterscarp be reached, where a final lodgment or crowning will be formed.

Defilade of the approaches.
In dealing with a small fortress or isolated work, it may be possible to direct the approaches in front of the parallels so as to be secure from enfilade; but with a girdle of forts on a large circle, even if they do not mutually flank the near foregrounds, the counter-approaches between them will do so, as in the case of the southern forts of Paris (pl. viii.); hence, in many cases, an advance by zigzags[1] will be impossible after a time, and this will, more than ever, drive the assailant to proceed by direct lines. As long as the exposure is not great, the advance is by common trenches; the sections of the tasks being the same as for the first parallel. As we near the fortress, the power the defender may have of illuminating the ground by electricity and light balls, added to the difficulty of keeping down his fire at night, may now, in some cases, make it easier to work by day than night. In this way, at Strassburg in 1870, the French fire was so kept down in the day-time, that flying sap was used throughout in the advanced attack. Before Charleston, in 1863, saps were carried on in the day-time under musketry fire, and sometimes against the fire of the artillery, though the latter generally stopped them.[2] In any case, to *The saps.* get cover early, common or flying sap must be used; and the latter, on account of its greater quickness, will be employed, whenever possible, in the further advance.

The difficulty is the weight of the common gabion, two of which cannot be carried far. Accordingly, the Austrians[3] propose a carrying party, who each brings up one gabion and go forward as a covering

---
[1] By a slight mistake in tracing an approach at Strassburg in 1870, it was laid open to the French, and several men and officers in it were killed.

[2] Gillmore, p. 213. [3] Brunner.

party, while each of the working party brings up a second gabion. The result is a constant confusion, as the parties get mixed. The Prussian plan is similar, but better arranged, as the carrying men are first retired before the workmen come up; but thus a double strength of men is turned out, and exposed at the most unfavourable moment.

We believe our plan to be the best, if pains be taken to make the gabions so light, that two can be carried up by one man in addition to his tools.

Very stiff gabions can be made of wire netting, combined with ordinary wicker work (figs. 37 and 38, pl. xxi.). Those 2 ft. 6 in. wide, weighing only 18 lbs. each, allow the men to adhere to the usual task, two paces long; though they can, of course, be made circular, like a common gabion, with even less weight.[1]

Light gabions.

The gabions would be brought up to the most advanced trench depôts, whence the parties would carry them to the tracing. The working parties would advance over the steps in the parallels, in working columns, and be extended by files, as already described; or, when they are small, and the work near the lodgment they start from, they can file out in single rank after the directing officer. In cases of great exposure, flying sap will be done by giving each man one of the service sap-shields,[2] or any available iron. These shields will also be very useful for general purposes, such as covering very exposed sentries. The Germans, at Mézières in 1870, used

Sap-shields.

---

[1] It is here worth remarking, that the wire netting for 1,000 gabions weighs about 1½ tons, as compared with 10 tons, the weight of the gabion bands for 1,000 band gabions; even, therefore, when the latter could not be brought up, the former might easily be carried. In the absence of wire netting, a light gabion may be made by substituting three sand-bags, or strips of carpet, canvas, or dry hay-bands.

[2] These are of steel, 3 ft. 6 in. × 1 ft. 9 in. × $\frac{1}{16}$ in., and weigh 54 lbs. As they are capable of resisting the 480-grain M. H. bullet, the penetration of which is, at least, as 11 to 8 compared with most small arms: it is a question whether a thinner and wider shield might not answer better. The Austrian steel shield is 3 ft. × 2 ft. × 0·2 in. Steel $\frac{1}{16}$ in., or iron $\frac{1}{8}$ in. thick, on 3 inches of hard wood backing, is bullet-proof.

plate-iron from a factory to make 500 feet of covered communication; and the French, at the second siege of Paris (1871), used plates of iron on timber, as shields across roads of approach.

By these methods the approaches may be carried forward to the second, and sometimes to the third parallel, by flying, or ordinary single sap. When, however, zigzags become impossible, the approaches may advance somewhat as in figs. 42 or 43, either by double flying, or double ordinary sap; the great advantage of the former being its rapid progress, and also that, with it, gabions are used; for, with the common deep saps, the difficulty of placing gabions, has now led to their disuse. Formerly, 3 ft. was considered deep enough for saps, but, owing to the greater use of curved and high-angle fire, and the formidable effects of shrapnel, a depth of 4 ft. is required in the flying sap, and of at least 4 ft. 6 in. in the common saps (figs. 41 and 36).[1] The advantage of this method is that the T heads act as traverses to the branches, and are therefore raised as high as possible; thus, a height of 5 ft. would give fair cover against a drop of 1 in 6 for a length of 30 feet of branch. When, however, it is desirable to make the branches longer, they must be blinded (figs. 42 and 51), and deepened from each traverse to the rear; one or two such blindages would allow the branch to be increased 30 to 60 ft.

It has been suggested that these straight approaches are defenceless against flank attacks; as, however, they will always be flanked by musketry from a parallel not over 300 yards from them, it does not seem necessary to make them wide enough to have steps; while in the case of night attacks, the guard of the trenches could stand, under shelter of the tra-

---

[1] The Prussian sap is 4 ft. 6 in., and the Austrian deep sap 6 ft. deep. The former is said to advance at from 4 to 5 feet an hour; the latter, according to Brunner, from 4 to 6 feet! Our experience with a sap of 4 ft. 6 in. is, that a progress of 4 feet an hour is unusually good. With the old 3-ft. saps 7 or 8 feet was a good rate, and when opposed to inferior arms, we should still use them to save time.

verses, on the central tongues, during the progress of the sap (fig. 51), and flank the advance of a sortie.

For regular sapping, the gabion, as well as the sap-roller, has been abandoned on the Continent. With increased depth in the sap, the difficulty of placing the first justifies its disuse; but the replacing of the sap-roller by an earthen parapet, constantly turned over, greatly delays progress; while the objection to the brushwood sap-roller, namely, its excessive weight of about three-quarters of a ton, and consequent clumsiness, may, it is thought, be got over. One substitute on favourable ground will be a pair of steel shields on some form of sloping frame on wheels. These, however, are apt to be displaced even by a heavy splinter, and in many cases we would prefer a sap-roller stuffed with cotton, and light enough to be lifted as well as rolled.[1] On rough ground, where nothing will roll, the earth cover to the sap-head might be replaced by a movable heap of sand-bags filled with cotton, each weighing only 8 or 10 lbs., and therefore easily thrown forward. Again, in cases of extreme exposure, portions of flying sap, and lodgments for riflemen may be formed by rolling up a line of sap-rollers, light enough to be manageable, and behind which men could work under musketry fire. Gabions filled with cotton would also

Sap-rollers.

Cotton stuffing.

[1] Cotton, even when not to be got from bedding, &c., can always be brought up, and when compressed is not bulky—a bale of 5 or 6 cwt. being only 5' × 3' × 1'. Loose cotton, stuffed by hand, weighs only 4 to 8 lbs. to a cubic foot; while, from the experiments mentioned by Gillmore (p. 253) on cotton in bags, the penetration of the rifled bullet into it appears to be only 22 inches, or twice that into sand: so that, weight for weight, it has about 9 times the resistance of the latter. The weights of 6-ft. sap-rollers, with wooden cylinders and cotton stuffing, would, for diameters of 2, 3, and 4 feet, be respectively about 220, 360, and 470 lbs.: so that, at need, they could easily be carried over parapets and rough places by two to four men, and they might be stuffed in the advanced trenches. Untwisted hawser strands, such as are used for mantlets, are also suitable: their weight is about 20 lbs. to a cubic foot, and a thickness of 6 in. is bullet-proof. A thickness of 3 in., stuffed between an outer and inner cylinder of brushwood, would make an efficient sap-roller of about the same weight as those stuffed with cotton. Both hemp and cotton can be made uninflammable, by a solution of chloride of calcium.

give immediate cover, and they and the rollers could be used elsewhere, when the parapet was thrown up. Steel shields, too, when available, will be put to a similar use.

The ordinary double sap with traverses is complicated, and being in one line is apt to be enfiladed for its whole length; while, for the methods shown in figs. 42 and 43, the branches might be done by single saps back to back, and the T end by flying sap, with sap-rollers, shields, or gabions; generally at night, and, if possible, beforehand, so as to screen the direction of the sap from the front: for which purpose, also, screens meant only to conceal may sometimes be used.

As the saps will suffer most from curved defensive fire from the outlying counter-batteries, they should, in general, be directed on the capital of the fort, so as to benefit by its shelter.

WAR OF MINES.

We have now to consider how the defenders' countermines must be dealt with. Mining is one of the earliest arts used in war, and new changes have only increased its importance; for instance, by arming it with powder, and more recently because it is a defensive resource which has not been impaired by the improvement in arms.[1] The slowness of its progress is the chief objection to mining. As far as expenditure of life is concerned, it is most economical. At Schweidnitz, where the assailant spent 47 days in

[1] A Memnonian bas-relief of 2000 B.C. shows the Egyptians, protected by mantlets, undermining a fortress wall; and Josephus (lib. vi., chap. vii.) mentions that Saul attacked the cities of the Amalekites with mines—"ὀρυγμασιν ὑπόνομοις." Polybius relates that the Persians took Chalcedon, by mining under it for a distance of 15 stadia; and Thucydides (lib. ii.) speaks of countermines at the siege of Platæa; while Cæsar complains (lib. vii.) that, at the siege of Avaricum, the Gauls, with their mines, would not let him build his agger "et aggerem cuniculis subtrahebant." Powder was first used in mining, by the Genoese, at the attack of Screzzanella in 1487.

mining, he only lost 25 men; while the French loss in mining at Sebastopol was only 45 men killed and wounded.

The defence has in its favour a prepared and organized system, with better means for earth-boring, for ventilation, and for drainage, &c.; but as it cannot afford to furnish the assailant with lodgments on the surface, it can only fire small charges, with a radius of destruction of about 20 feet, the partial effects extending about one-half further. It can also use small charges (fig. 47) so lodged as not to injure its own galleries, but to poison the earth and injure the assailant. The assailant, on the contrary, may use the largest charges. These enable him to destroy the defensive galleries, at a distance beyond the reach of the defenders' limit of destruction, and also to get the cover of large craters. If the ground be mined, a mine-lodgment like a demi-parallel is formed a little short of the supposed zone or *mine-field*. Here a blinded depôt of mining tools, and a magazine are formed, and supplies collected. The mine lodgments.

The methods of the attack are based on such knowledge of the countermines as can be obtained. They are:— Methods of attack.

1st. To drive galleries from the lodgment till within 25 to 35 feet of the countermines, and then fire overcharged mines of 7,000 to 8,000 lbs., which destroy the defenders' galleries to a distance of 50 or 60 feet, and form craters of 65 to 95 feet.[1] These craters should not, if possible, blow in the mine lodgment, but should overlap each other. In any case they are at once occupied, and crowned by a rude flying sap, and connected with the rear. From these lodgments, galleries are advanced, and fresh ground gained.

2nd. Instead of driving galleries, when speed is required, or the earth is poisoned, to use large earth augers, boring to a depth of 20 feet or so from the mine-lodgment, or craters; as the hole they make is only 9 to 12 in. in diameter, charges of cotton are fired in them instead of powder. The surface effect Gun-cotton.

[1] A charge of old powder of 7,700 lbs. fired at Graudenz in 1873, with a L. L. R. of 25·3 ft. made a crater of 94 ft. in diameter.

of gun-cotton in earth is small, but experiments have shown that its lateral effect is at least $2\frac{1}{2}$ times that of powder. We are, therefore, bound to use it, whenever we shall not be hindered by its after effects on our own operations, and when the destruction of the defenders' galleries is more important than the formation of large craters.

3rd. To make a hasty lodgment above the defenders' galleries, whence shafts are sunk at 1 or 2 lined intervals, and at the bottoms of these, to fire heavy charges of cotton or powder, so as to crush the galleries below,[1] and cause the loss of the advanced parts. This method is evidently attended with much risk of failure, but shortens the operation, and in the long run saves lives. The French, in the operations before the Bastion du Mât, at Sebastopol, fired charges at the bottom of shafts in this way, but without much effect.

4th. To drive a shallow gallery in the place of the lodgment, and fire charges along it to destroy galleries below, and provide a safe lodgment. This was done with partial success by the French before the Bastion du Mât, where they fired 23,940 kilos. of powder in 17 charges, about 10 metres apart. A trench was thus opened, except where some charges failed, but a stratum of rock saved the Russian mines beneath. With this object it has been suggested that charges of gun-cotton should be laid bare on the ground, so as, when fired, to make a surface lodgment.[2]

There are a few of the details of mining we would wish to touch on, these are:—

Ventilation of mines.

1st. The necessity of providing proper means of ventilation.

In the galleries of the attack, with a rapid fall inwards, the carbonic acid from respiration collects at the head, and a method of exhaustion is therefore necessary. Again, in working in poisoned earth the great danger is from carbonic oxide, 1 or 2 per cent. of

---

[1] Niel.

[2] A charge of 500 lbs. of gun-cotton, fired on the surface of the ground, has been noticed to make a crater of a diameter of 22 feet and 3 ft. 6 in. deep.

which is fatal, though it does not interfere with the burning of lights. Here, then, this light gas must be expelled by the influx, *under pressure*, of fresh air from beyond the entrance. Turbines fail in providing enough pressure, and bellows in giving enough quantity, because, for the attack, hand-power alone is available. There are, however, several forms of pressure-blower in use in this country which promise to suit our purpose, as they either exhaust air, or, when reversed, impel it with pressure (figs. 54 and 55, pl. xxii.).[1] *Air engines.*

Further, the plan of a face mask (figs. 50, 52, and 57), which enables a man to breathe pure air through a stiff 1-inch flexible pipe as far as 70 to 80 feet from the entrance, is excellent; and a number of these, with their pipes, &c., would be all that is wanted of this kind for the short attack galleries; though a few compressed air knapsacks (fig. 26, pl. xx.), and a pump are desirable additions to the siege mining equipment, in case of having to deal with complicated or captured galleries,[2] the more so as the pump can be used to supply air to the wearer of a face mask when the distance is too great for the use of the pipe alone. *Respirators.*

2nd. The necessity of combining Ord's hose, and a short length of Bickford's fuse, with all electrical arrangements for firing.

3rd. The provision of bomb-proof porches over all entrances to galleries.

4th. The use of sun-dried bricks, and logs of wood in default of sand-bags for tamping. We can seldom reckon on sand-bags for this purpose, though with them, the small galleries can be tamped at the rate of nearly a foot a minute.

5th. The desirableness of testing the new pebble powders, to see how far the surface effects are in-

---

[1] The lightest, of 84 lbs., can be worked by one man, and gives a blast of 60 c. f. a minute; those of 4 cwt., worked by four men, give 150 c. f. Stiff india-rubber hose must be used, and the pressure can be varied by having nozzles of different sizes.

[2] Of these knapsacks, twelve are provided in our "Siege Equipment;" but apparently no pump.

creased by using them, and whether the lateral effects are altered.

Mining cases.

6th. While believing that the dimensions of our mining galleries are, without exception, the best, we think the pattern of case might be improved. The necessity of leaving a space over a corner is inconvenient, if not unsafe, and those who have mined with their own hands, know the loss of time that occurs in just fitting in the last corner of an *obstinate* case. If we did away with top tenons (fig. 44), and let No. 1 jam the sides roughly into place, at the top, by a screw compressor; the other Nos. could make alterations, if required, at a convenient distance in rear of No. 1, and add top battens, with a crushing resistance as great as the cross breaking resistance of the side pieces (fig. 48). This would save the time of No. 1, on whom the rate of progress depends, and would support the earth so effectually that, with cases at intervals, the intermediate earth roof would arch itself, like the brick arches between girders: so that with fewer cases we should have greater safety than at present. The compressors might also be used, on an emergency, to strengthen the heads of galleries when an explosion is feared.

Mining machines.

We cannot leave the subject of mining, without noticing the attempts that have been made to obtain by means of steam used directly, or through the medium of compressed air, a greater rate of progress than the miner can maintain. So far, these have not succeeded: had they done so, bearing in mind the difficulty of using steam in so exposed a position as the mine lodgment, the balance of advantage would, it is thought, have rested with the defence. For the attack, the use of a mining machine which appears most feasible, is to apply it to work an auger, at a rapid rate, and fit to make a hole of sufficient size to take a fair charge of gun-cotton, the chamber being, if necessary, enlarged by firing a few very small charges in it beforehand. By constantly driving these in front of their work, the attack could ward off the defenders' strokes, and progress both more quickly, and with less loss.

Space does not permit us to enter into the details of the further advance of the saps to the counterscarp; but they can now be arranged with greater simplicity, owing to their being uncomplicated in most cases by artillery arrangements, and, combined with this, they will have less width, greater depth, and more overhead cover.

When the counterscarp wall is reached, it may be necessary to blow it in with over-charged mines, either to render the artillery problem more easy, or to fill up the ditch, as was done at Schweidnitz, where the explosion formed a practicable ramp against the escarp; or, again, to smother or mask the low flanking defences of the ditch. In cases where curved fire or the use of gun-cotton bombs has failed to silence these latter, or to breach the detached wall or escarp, mines may, with these objects, be carried under the ditch. In general the counterscarp wall will be cut through by hand or by using gun-cotton, and covered passages will be made across the ditch. *Demolition of counterscarp.*

As it is now no longer necessary, as a rule, to provide means for bringing guns into the ditch by great or blinded galleries, and as these have always presented great difficulties; it is believed, that the counterscarp can now be reached most surely, by a number of common galleries three feet wide, if necessary, which can be driven close together, at known rates, and in much less time than it takes to drive the great or blinded galleries;[1] though in a case like that at Lunette 53 at Strassburg, where there is no counterscarp wall, and where a comparatively shallow open cutting can be made and roofed, the blinded gallery is less objectionable, and a roof of rails, as used there, is desirable. When these galleries reach the wall, returns should be made behind it; the galleries should be tamped and shored till the wall is blown in; and when the breach is formed, and the caponiers silenced, they should be opened, and used to give a large front, either to assaulting columns, or to working parties employed to pass down earth or fascines for filling up *Small galleries of descent.*

---

[1] P. P. R. E., vol. xix., p. 36.

still water ditches, or small piers of metal-lined cases, powder barrels, &c., for bridging running water, and filled sand-bags or cotton-bags for parapets. In this case, as 2 or 3 feet is hardly wide enough, the miners that follow No. 1 could form recesses for a chain of men on each side, who could stand in them and pass down what is required; the formation of these need not delay the progress of the galleries (fig. 49).

The preparation for the assault will, of course, be made by the greatest possible amount of fire on the breaches, and the interior of the works, where the defenders will have prepared covered blindages for the reserves who are to resist assault; but, in addition, a belief seems to be afloat, that both then and earlier, means must be found for throwing in large masses of the new explosives, which by the shock of their detonation, will clear away everything in their neighbourhood.

Earth mortars. We have heard lately of *sarartines* or shell-fougasses, but the statement that they carry dynamite must be accepted with suspicion. Wet gun-cotton, however, is a perfectly fit material, and it is only a question as to how the largest charges can be just carried into the work. Very large mortars, cause their shells to bury themselves too deep if fired from a distance, though they may yet be forthcoming in a form available for close quarters. In their absence, the means to use are either a powder rocket acting as a vehicle, or an earth mortar formed by revetting the sides of a hole in the ground. If the first can be got to work, it is believed it would, on the whole, answer best. If not, deep holes in the ground, lined with wrought-iron tubes in quadrants (figs. 53 and 56), will act as mortars, and might throw wrought-iron shells, made in segments for transport, and strengthened inside with flanges, so as to carry 600 or 700 lbs. of gun-cotton [1] (figs. 45 and 46). The ex-

---

[1] Wooden cylinders over 700 lbs. in weight have been fired on the Continent, from holes lined with battens, with charges of about $\frac{1}{8}$th the weight of the shell, they ranged for distances over 350 yards,

plosion of one of these against a detached wall (fig. 39) would rarely fail to breach it, while a few of them would wreck the interiors of most works.

CONCLUSIONS.

In the foregoing remarks the attempt has been made, not so much to give a detailed description of the successive steps in a siege, as to dwell on those features which in these days have, perforce, been subject to the widest changes; and, further, by the light of recent experience, to point out what appears to be the drift of the changes we may expect in the near future.

The general result, as regards the attack of fortresses, may, it is thought, be summed up as follows, namely, that the different stages will be:— *Stages of the attack.*

First Stage. An investment; conceived secretly, completed promptly, maintained rigidly.

For the first is wanted unity of command; for the second, good information and mobility in all arms; for the third, aptness in applying all the arts of field fortification, and in developing to the utmost the retaining power of the new arms; in using the power of rapid concentration that is given by the field telegraph; and in employing the means of transport and supply afforded by steam.

Second Stage. The selection of the front or fronts of attack.

The approval of a siege plan.

The preparation of the siege parks, and particularly of the communications to and from them by railroads or roads.

The bringing up of the siege trains.

The collection of the local siege materials, and the use of steam for the preparation of the timber work.

The pushing forward and strengthening of the line of investment; as well as the commencement of the

---

and had an initial velocity of over 170 feet. Both the shells and their time fuses were fired by electricity. They only went about twelve inches into the ground on falling.

earliest siege works out of sight of the defenders, and, as far as possible, without their knowledge.

Third Stage. The completion of the first artillery position, at a distance from the fortress, which, roughly speaking, will be more than three times as great as in the days of smooth bores.

The arming of the batteries.

The opening and maintenance of the first bombardment, protected by a covering force.

The fights for the intermediate localities, under cover of the bombardment.

The gradual confinement of the defenders within the zone of the musketry fire of the place.

Fourth Stage. The establishment of the attack in an infantry position extending along the borders of the musketry zone of the defences, enveloping, as far as possible, the fronts attacked and the area of the further advance, and composed of existing and artificial cover, as well as provided with covered communications to the depôts in rear.

Further, the construction of a second artillery position in the neighbourhood of, and protected by the first parallel—whence, in great measure, the work of destruction to be carried on by the guns, will be effected.

Fifth Stage. The further advance (along the most direct lines) of approaches provided with overhead cover, against the searching power of modern shells.

The protection of these approaches, at convenient intervals, by additional parallels and lodgments; and the complete suppression of the defenders' fire by the constant use of light guns, mortars, wall-pieces and musketry.

Sixth Stage. The war of mines, by which a final advance to the counterscarp is made; or, in their absence, the advance thereto by sapping.

The crowning of the crest of the glacis.

The breaching of the escarps, and silencing of the caponiers by distant artillery fire, aided by observations from the near approaches, and by the miners' advance to, and demolition of the counterscarps and caponiers when necessary.

Seventh Stage. The expulsion of the garrison from the neighbourhood of the breaches, by bringing the fire of all available arms to bear thereon; and further perhaps by the use of masses of gun-cotton, carried in by rockets or by earth mortars.

The passage of the ditches by the ordinary methods, and the simultaneous assault *in force* of all the breaches; followed by the capture of the work or works.

Eighth Stage. The armament of the gorges of the captured works, the connection of them by telegraph, and the use of them as keeps in a new base of attack against any further defences, the advance against which is carried out on the same principles.

Such, it is believed, is the state of things we must prepare for.

The successful conduct of such enterprises must depend :— Conditions for success.

1st. On the numerical fitness of the force employed.

2nd. On the moral and physical qualities of all arms.

3rd. On the technical knowledge of the special troops.

4th. On the state of national preparation, as regards arms and materials.

For the first, rules must always be qualified by the circumstances of each case, particularly when, as in the war of 1870-71, the widest differences may exist between the troops engaged.

For the second, we must remember that the soldier hates trouble; and though, in the excitement of a fight, great efforts may be relied on, the monotony of the work, and the severity[1] of the labour of a siege will always be distasteful. Hence discipline, combined with the personal influence and exertion of the officers, can alone secure the execution of the works with such promptness as the physical fitness of the men permits.

---

[1] Towards the end of the siege of Strassburg in 1870-71, so exhausted were the men, that the reliefs, in returning from work, preferred to cross the open, under fire, rather than march a few yards further to gain cover.

For the third, it is necessary that the technical troops should practice in peace all that they will have to do in war, and under conditions approaching those of war as nearly as possible.

That the artillery should have put their weapons to the exact uses they will have to put them to at a siege.

That the engineers, while learning from their peace employment the best ways of conducting works,[1] should, in conjunction with the other arms, and away from the facilities provided at head-quarters, have opportunities of executing every form of field and siege work.

Lastly, in these days when war is declared by *post*, but begun by *telegraph*, there is often scant time for getting ready; and not only should our ideas be matured, but our men and materials should be ready too.

In this peace-loving country, happy in being free from the thirst for conquest, it may be objected that fighting only concerns us in reference to self-defence: even so, the best preparation for defence is the study of the attack; but a nation that rules nearly a fourth of the inhabitants of the globe—most of them too on the sole condition of readiness for offensive war—cannot calculate for ever on freedom from the necessity for it, a freedom that all history shows, is never unlimited; while from the same source we learn, that fitness for offensive war is the best security for peace, and that the most matured wisdom dictated the saying—

"Si vis pacem, para bellum."

---

[1] From their experience in the conduct of work, the American engineers at the siege of Charleston showed, it is thought, more originality of design, and more boldness in execution than the Germans did in all the sieges of the war of 1870-71.

AINS.[1]

	RIAN. (400 guns each.)		ITALIAN. (One train of 200 guns.)				REMARKS.
Proportion in train.	Weight.		Description and Calibre of pieces.	Proportion in train.	Weight.		
	Gun cwts.	Shell lbs.			Gun cwts.	Shell lbs.	
1 in 20	95·91	192·6	22 c. M. L. R. Mortar .	1 in 6·6	89·4	205	[1] The details of the foreign trains are extracted from the "Jahresberichte" of 1874.
1 in 20	40·14	85	16 c. M. L. R. Gun . .	1 in 3·3	60·5	65	
1 in 4	63	65·4	12 c. M. L. R. Bronze Gun	1 in 2	14·4	24·5	[2] The 64-pr. M. L. R. Gun will also have a 90 lbs. battering shell.
1 in 4	30	60·8	15 c. S. B. Mortars . .	1 in 20			
1 in 10	29·1	35·5					[3] To be replaced by 21 c. B. L. R. Howitzers. Some of the 15 c. Guns are to be ring-guns.
1 in 10	12·8	17·7					
1 in 10	—	—					
1 in 10	—	—					
rifled) . . 36·48 cwt.			Mean weight per piece (rifled) . . 38·76 cwt.				[4] These mean weights are the total weights of metal, divided by the total numbers in the train.
ditto . . 50·75 lbs.			Mean weight of shell ditto . . 62·5 lbs.				
with different shells 5			Number of rifled pieces with different shells 3				
ided per gun . .			Number of rounds provided per gun . 500 to 975				

each of the two units.

For the third, it is necessary that the technical troops should practice in peace all that they will have to do in war, and under conditions approaching those of war as nearly as possible.

That the artillery should have put their weapons to the exact uses they will have to put them to at a siege.

That the engineers, while learning from their peace employment the best ways of conducting works,[1] should, in conjunction with the other arms, and away from the facilities provided at head-quarters, have opportunities of executing every form of field and siege work.

Lastly, in these days when war is declared by *post*, but begun by *telegraph*, there is often scant time for getting ready; and not only should our ideas be matured, but our men and materials should be ready too.

In this peace-loving country, happy in being free from the thirst for conquest, it may be objected that fighting only concerns us in reference to self-defence: even so, the best preparation for defence is the study of the attack; but a nation that rules nearly a fourth of the inhabitants of the globe—most of them too on the sole condition of readiness for offensive war—cannot calculate for ever on freedom from the necessity for it, a freedom that all history shows, is never unlimited; while from the same source we learn, that fitness for offensive war is the best security for peace, and that the most matured wisdom dictated the saying—

"Si vis pacem, para bellum."

---

[1] From their experience in the conduct of work, the American engineers at the siege of Charleston showed, it is thought, more originality of design, and more boldness in execution than the Germans did in all the sieges of the war of 1870-71.

APPENDIX A.

TABLE OF REVISED EUROPEAN SIEGE TRAINS.[1]

BRITISH.

(Equal proportions of light and heavy units.)[2]

Description and Calibre of piece.	Proportion in train.	Weight: Gun cwts.	Weight: Shell lbs.
[illegible] M. L. R. Gun	[illegible]	[illegible]	[illegible]
[illegible] Gun	[illegible]	[illegible]	[illegible]
[illegible] M. L. R. [illegible]	[illegible]	[illegible]	[illegible]
[illegible] M. L. R. Gun	[illegible]	[illegible]	[illegible]
[illegible] M. L. R.	[illegible]	[illegible]	[illegible]

Mean weight[3] per piece (rifled)	[illegible] cwt.
Mean weight of shell ditto	[illegible] lbs.
Number of rifled pieces with different shells	[illegible]
Number of rounds provided per gun	[illegible]

PRUSSIAN.

(Two trains of 400 guns each.)

Description and Calibre of piece.	Proportion in train.	Weight: Gun cwts.	Weight: Shell lbs.
[illegible] B. L. R. Mortar*	1 in 10	[illegible]	[illegible]
[illegible] Long B. L. R. Gun	[illegible]	[illegible]	[illegible]
[illegible] Short do. Gun	[illegible]	[illegible]	[illegible]
[illegible] B. L. R. Gun	[illegible]	[illegible]	[illegible]
[illegible] B. L. R. Gun	[illegible]	[illegible]	[illegible]
[illegible] S. B. Mortars	[illegible]		—
[illegible] Wall Pieces	[illegible]	[illegible]	[illegible]

Mean weight per piece (rifled)	[illegible] cwt.
Mean weight of shell ditto	[illegible] lbs.
Number of rifled pieces with different shells	[illegible]
Number of rounds provided per gun	[illegible]

RUSSIAN.

(Two trains of 400 guns each.)

Description and Calibre of piece.	Proportion in train.	Weight: Gun cwts.	Weight: Shell lbs.
[illegible] B. L. R. Mortar	1 in 10	[illegible]	[illegible]
[illegible] do.	[illegible]	[illegible]	[illegible]
[illegible] Long B. L. R. Gun	[illegible]	[illegible]	[illegible]
[illegible] Short do. Gun	[illegible]	[illegible]	[illegible]
[illegible] B. L. R. Gun	[illegible]	[illegible]	[illegible]
S. B. Mortars	1 in 10	—	[illegible]
Do. do.	[illegible]	—	[illegible]

Mean weight per piece (rifled)	[illegible]
Mean weight of shell ditto	[illegible] lbs.
Number of rifled pieces with different shells	[illegible]
Number of rounds provided per gun	[illegible]

AUSTRIAN.

(Two trains of 400 guns each.)

Description and Calibre of piece.	Proportion in train.	Weight: Gun cwts.	Weight: Shell lbs.
[illegible] B. L. R. Mortar	[illegible]	[illegible]	[illegible]
[illegible] do. do.	[illegible]	[illegible]	[illegible]
[illegible] Long B. L. R. Gun	[illegible]	[illegible]	[illegible]
[illegible] Short B. L. R. do.	[illegible]	[illegible]	[illegible]
[illegible] B. L. R. Gun	[illegible]	[illegible]	[illegible]
[illegible] do. do.	[illegible]	[illegible]	[illegible]
[illegible] S. B. Mortar	[illegible]	—	—
[illegible] do.	[illegible]	—	—

Mean weight per piece (rifled)	[illegible] cwt.
Mean weight of shell ditto	[illegible] lbs.
Number of rifled pieces with different shells	[illegible]
Number of rounds provided per gun	[illegible]

ITALIAN.

(One train of [illegible] guns.)

Description and Calibre of piece.	Proportion in train.	Weight: Gun cwts.	Weight: Shell lbs.
[illegible] M. L. R. Mortar	[illegible]	[illegible]	[illegible]
[illegible] M. L. R. Gun	[illegible]	[illegible]	[illegible]
[illegible] M. L. R. Bronze Gun	[illegible]	[illegible]	[illegible]
[illegible] S. B. Mortars	[illegible]		

Mean weight per piece (rifled)	[illegible] cwt.
Mean weight of shell ditto	[illegible] lbs.
Number of rifled pieces with different shells	[illegible]
Number of rounds provided per gun	[illegible]

REMARKS.

[1] The details of the foreign trains are [illegible] of [illegible].

[2] The large M. L. R. Gun will also have a [illegible] shell.

* To be replaced by [illegible] B. L. R. Howitzers. [illegible] are to be [illegible] guns.

[3] These mean weights are the actual weights of metal, divided by the total numbers in the train.

* [illegible] M. L. R. guns of [illegible] lbs., to be used as [illegible] or mortars, have since been added to each of the two units.

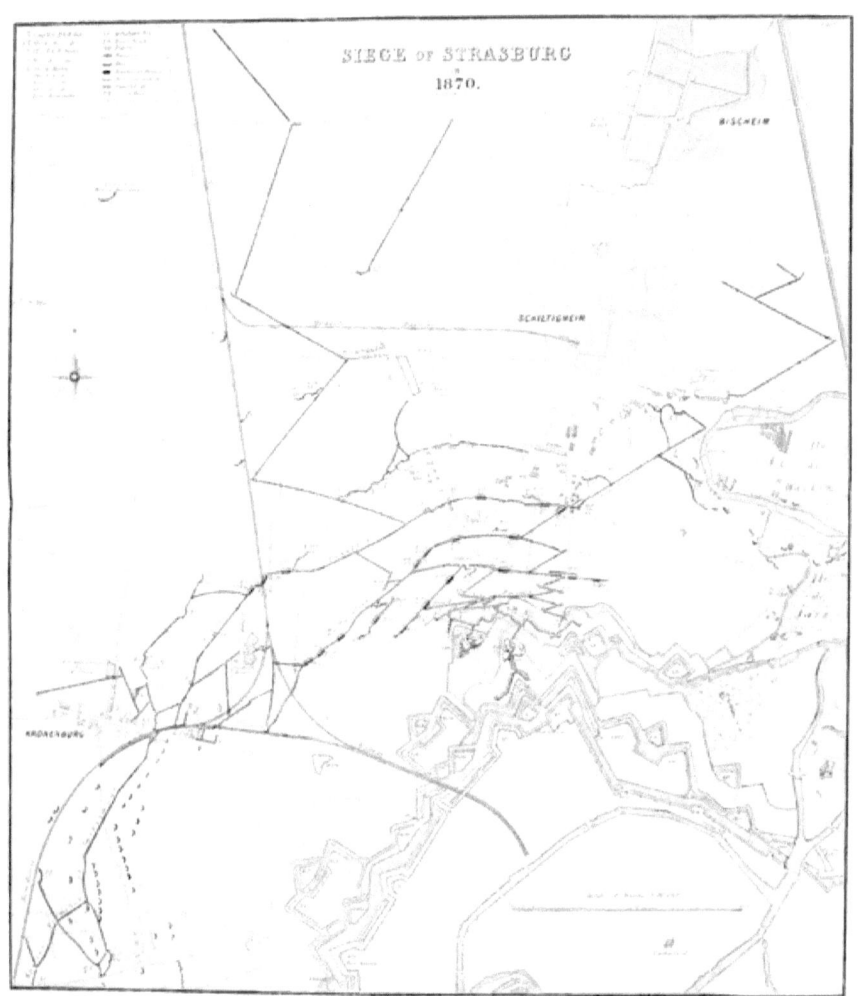

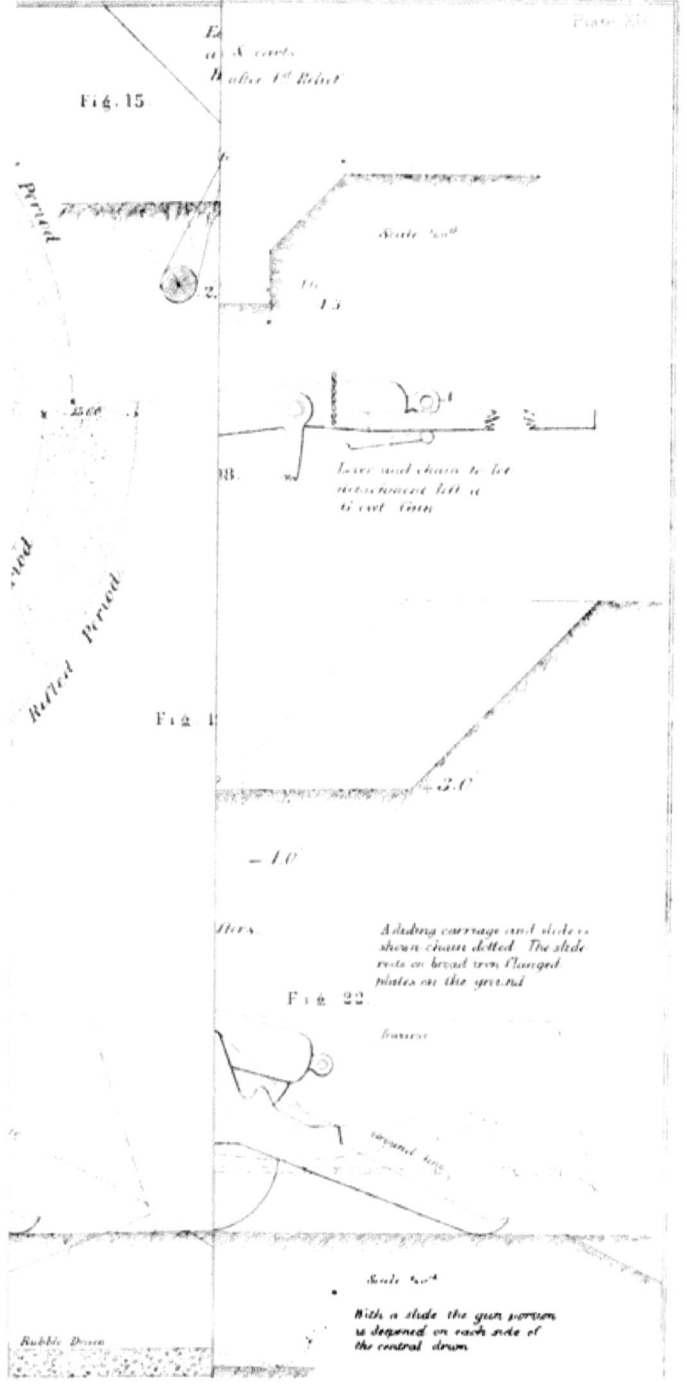

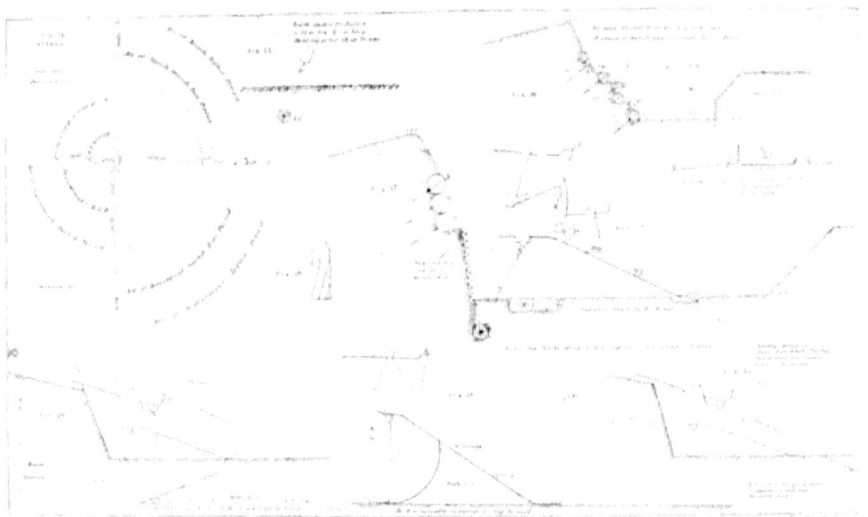

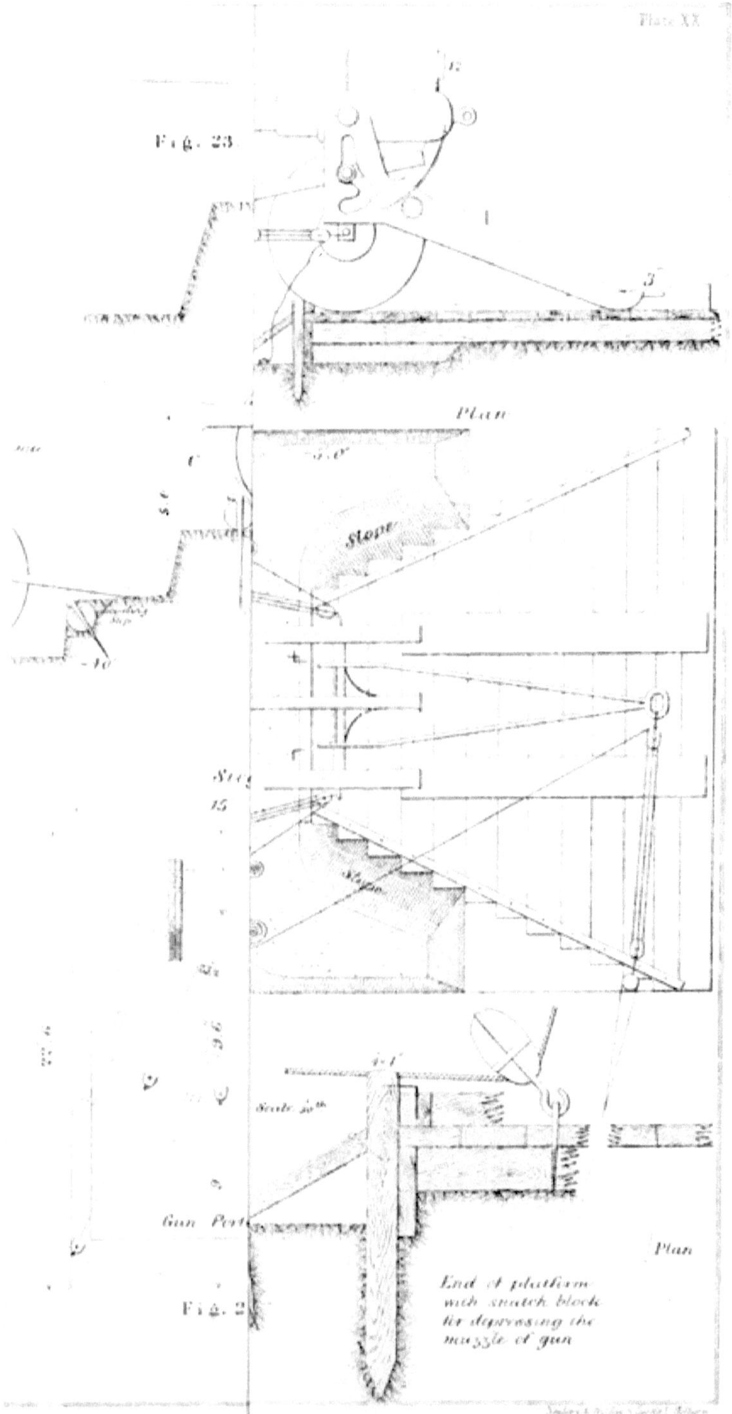
Plate XX
Fig. 23
Plan
Slope
Slope
Gun Port
Scale 1/20th
Plan
End of platform
with snatch block
for depressing the
muzzle of gun
Fig. 2

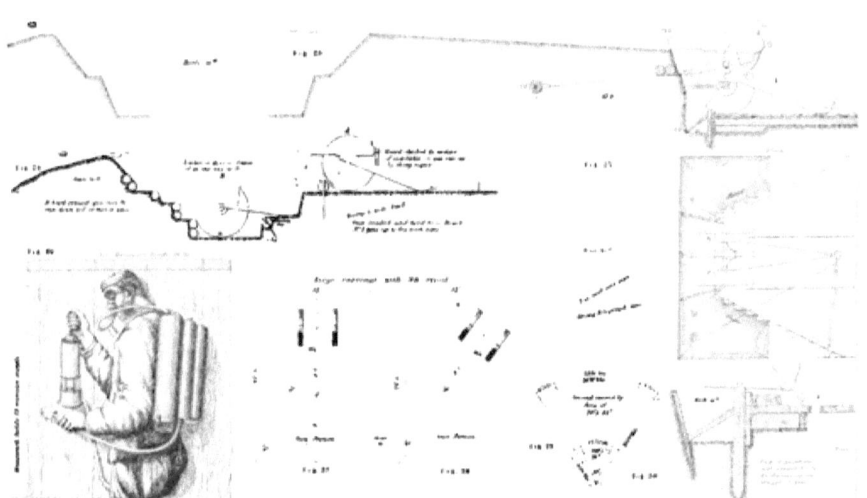

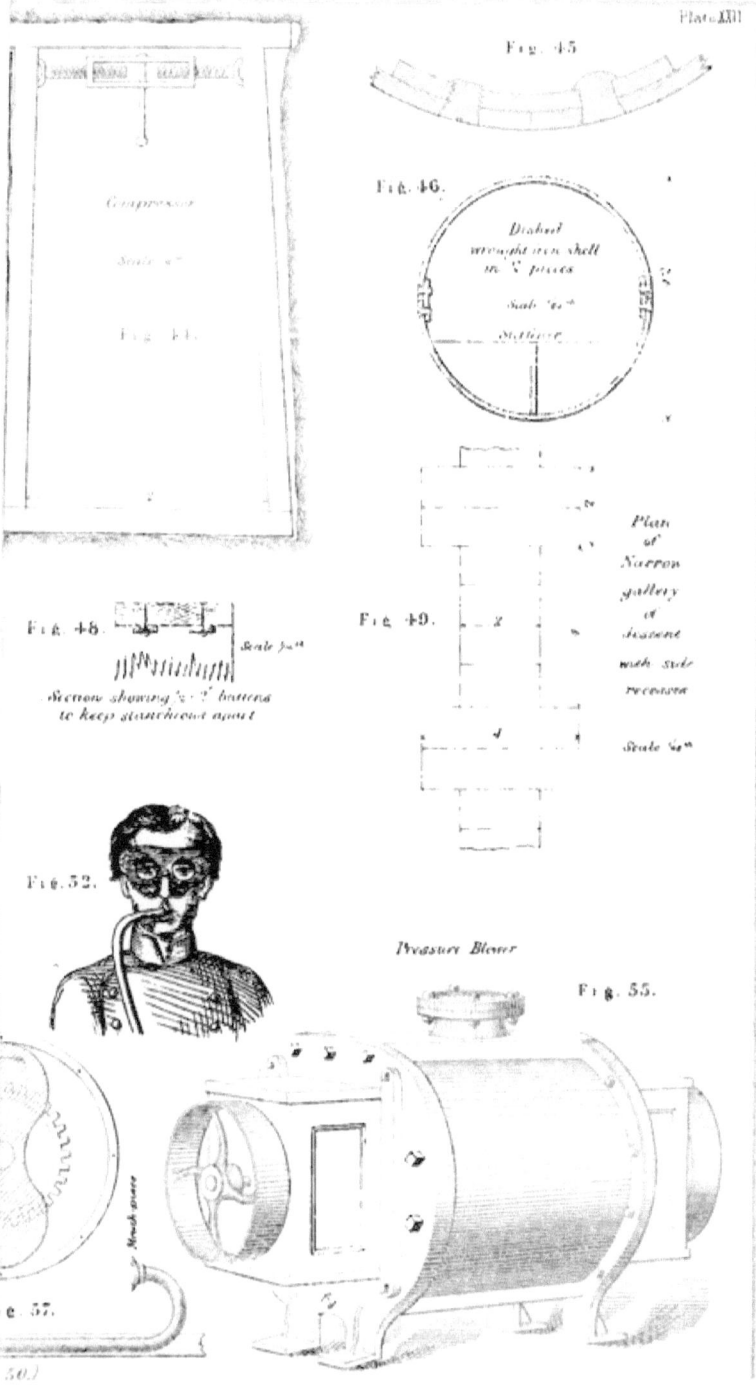

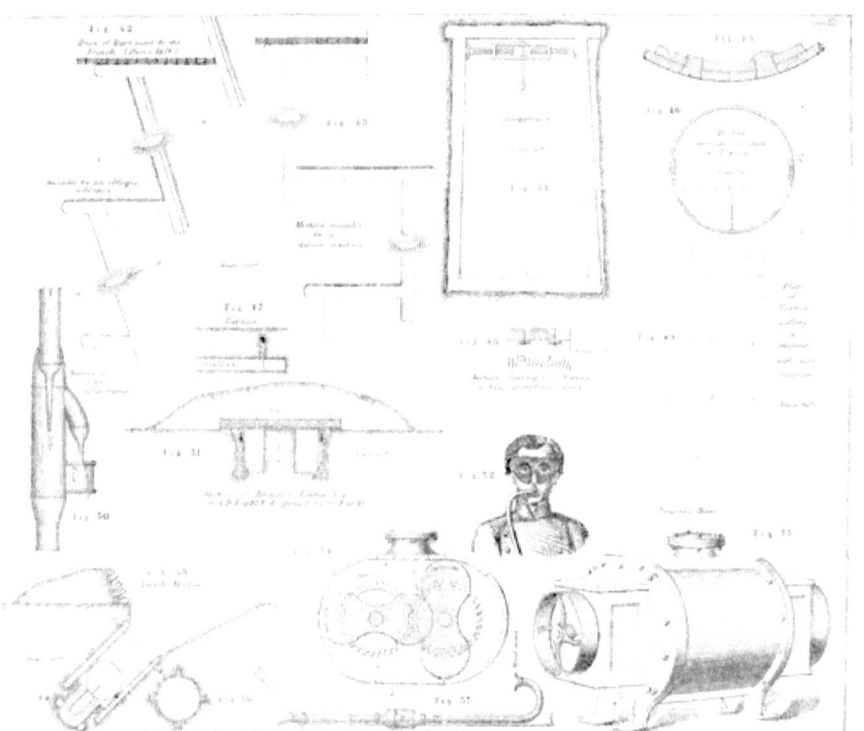

www.ingramcontent.com/pod-product-compliance
Lightning Source LLC
Chambersburg PA
CBHW020255170426
43202CB00008B/382